HERBERT MARCUSE
PHILOSOPHER OF UTOPIA
a graphic biography

NICK THORKELSON

PAUL BUHLE AND ANDREW T. LAMAS, EDITORS

City Lights Books | San Francisco

My thanks to Paul Buhle, who put this all together, and Andy Lamas, keeper of the flame; Marcuse family members Frances and Harold Marcuse, Osha and Rachel Neumann, and especially Peter Marcuse; the International Herbert Marcuse Society; former Marcuse graduate students Lowell Bergman, Andrew Feenberg, George Katsiaficas, and William Leiss; and my wife and daughter, Cynthia Bargar and Ruby Thorkelson, who were with me every inch.
—Nick Thorkelson

Portions of "Chapter Five: Eros and Brandeis" appeared previously in Pangyrus 5: The Resistance Issue (www.pangyrus.com).

Library of Congress Cataloging-in-Publication Data

Names: Thorkelson, Nick, author.
Title: Herbert Marcuse, philosopher of utopia : a graphic biography / Nick
  Thorkelson.
Description: San Francisco, CA : City Lights Books, [2019] | Includes
  bibliographical references and index.
Identifiers: LCCN 2018052494 | ISBN 9780872867857 (alk. paper)
Subjects: LCSH: Marcuse, Herbert, 1898-1979—Comic books, strips, etc. |
  Philosophers—United States—Biography—Comic books, strips, etc. |
  Graphic novels.
Classification: LCC B945.M2984 T46 2019 | DDC 191 [B] —dc23
LC record available at https://lccn.loc.gov/2018052494

City Lights Books are published at the City Lights Bookstore
261 Columbus Avenue, San Francisco, CA 94133
www.citylights.com

CONTENTS

Foreword *by Angela Y. Davis* v

Chapter One Assimilation & Catastrophe 1

Chapter Two The Sorrows of Young Marcuse 6

Chapter Three Fascists & Frankfurters 17

Chapter Four The Swine of 117th Street 28

Chapter Five Eros & Brandeis 47

Chapter Six The Reluctant Guru 69

Chapter Seven Step By Step 85

Afterword *by Andrew T. Lamas* 107

Further Reading 117

FOREWORD
Angela Y. Davis

As I write this preface in May 2018, in the city of Paris, French students and workers are conducting demonstrations, sit-ins, and occupations with the aim of challenging the Macron government's harsh attacks on labor and its announced efforts to restrict access to higher education. These protests reflect a growing consciousness of deepening structural inequalities in the Global North—especially for people of color, immigrants from the South, and more generally, poor and working class communities suffering the effects of global capitalism.

As if to accentuate the significance of the publication this year of the graphic biography, *Herbert Marcuse, Philosopher of Utopia*, these demonstrations in Paris coincide with the fiftieth anniversary of the 1968 student/worker uprisings, with which his utopian ideas have been historically associated. But serendipitously, Marcuse was in fact in Paris during the 1968 protests, attending, along with Lucien Goldmann and others, a United Nations Educational, Scientific and Cultural Organization (UNESCO) conference on Marx. Students who had occupied the École des Beaux Arts recognized him as he walked back to his hotel from the conference and invited him to speak to the assembly. When he addressed them, he brought greetings from the developing movement in the United States and, according to Andrew Feenberg, who accompanied him, praised the students for their critiques of capitalist consumerism.[1]

In 1968, I was one of Herbert Marcuse's graduate students at UC San Diego, and we all benefited both from his deep knowledge of European philosophical traditions and from the fearless way he manifested his solidarity with movements challenging military aggression, academic repression, and pervasive racism. Marcuse counseled us always to acknowledge the important differences between the realms of philosophy and political activism, as well as the complex relation between theory and radical social transformation. At the same time, he never failed to remind us that the most meaningful dimension of philosophy was its utopian element. "When truth cannot be realized within the established social order, it always appears to the latter as mere utopia."[2] As new generations of scholars and activists ponder the role of intellectuals in shaping radical movements of this era, I believe that Marcuse's ideas can be as valuable today as they were fifty years ago.

1. Andrew Feenberg, "Remembering Marcuse," in Herbert Marcuse, *Philosophy, Psychoanalysis and Emancipation*, Collected Papers of Herbert Marcuse, vol. 5, ed. Douglas Kellner and Clayton Pierce. (London: Routledge, 2011), 235-236.

2. Herbert Marcuse, "Philosophy and Critical Theory," trans. Jeremy J. Shapiro, in *Negations: Essays in Critical Theory* (Boston: Beacon Press, 1968), 143.

Shortly before the death of his longtime Frankfurt School colleague Theodor W. Adorno, Marcuse urgently debated with him the significance of the student movement. The focal point of their sometime intense exchange was Adorno's justification of the fact that the police were called in response to a student occupation of the Institute for Social Research. In criticizing this reliance on the police, Marcuse insisted that "if the alternative is the police or left-wing students, then I am with the students. . . . I still believe that our cause . . . is better taken up by the rebellious students than by the police."[3] Marcuse pointed out that even as he rejected the "unmediated translation of theory into praxis," he recognized that theory can be advanced by praxis and that although student activism of that period was neither unfolding within a revolutionary situation, nor even, he insisted, in a "pre-revolutionary one," it demanded recognition of new possibilities of emancipation.[4] It brought in, he said, some much needed fresh air when the world was suffocating in so many ways. "It is the air that we . . . also want to breathe some day, and it is certainly not the air of the establishment."[5]

While Marcuse did not always agree with particular tactics of radical movements of that era, he was very clear about the extent to which calls for black liberation, peace, gender justice, and for the restructuring of education represented important emancipatory tendencies of the era and, indeed, helped to push theory in progressive directions. *An Essay on Liberation and Counterrevolution and Revolt*, as well as his 1974 Stanford University lecture on "Marxism and Feminism," offers us evidence of his own efforts to engage directly with ideas associated with movements of that period.[6] His reference to "feminist socialism" in the latter essay predicted the important influence of anti-capitalist and anti-racist feminism on many contemporary movements, including prison abolition, campaigns against police violence, and justice for people with disabilities. The explicitly utopian dimension of Marcuse's thought attracted young intellectuals and activists during the historical conjuncture we associate with the uprisings of 1968. Fifty years later, as we confront the persisting globalities of slavery and colonialism, along with evolving structures of racial capitalism, Herbert Marcuse's ideas continue to reveal important lessons. The insistence on imagining emancipatory futures, even under the most desperate of circumstances, remains—Marcuse teaches us—a decisive element of both theory and practice.

3. Herbert Marcuse, in Theodor W. Adorno and Herbert Marcuse, "Correspondence on the German Student Movement," trans. Esther Leslie, *New Left Review* I/233 (January-February 1999), 125.

4. Ibid. Marcuse also wrote to Adorno: "You know me well enough to know that I reject the unmediated translation of theory into praxis just as emphatically as you do. But I do believe that there are situations, moments, in which theory is pushed on further by praxis—situations and moments in which theory that is kept separate from praxis becomes untrue to itself." Marcuse, "Correspondence," 125.

5. Ibid.

6. See Herbert Marcuse, *An Essay on Liberation* (Boston: Beacon Press, 1969); Herbert Marcuse, *Counterrevolution and Revolt* (Boston: Beacon Press, 1972); and, Herbert Marcuse, "Marxism and Feminism," *Women's Studies* 2.3 (1974), 279-288.

SPRING 1965, OAKLAND, CALIFORNIA:

IT'S BEAUTIFUL! THE UNIFICATION OF THE POLITICAL PRINCIPLE WITH THE PLEASURE PRINCIPLE!

WE HAVE NO RIGHT TO DESPAIR. THERE COULD BE GOOD THINGS OUT THERE AS MUCH AS WE'RE WILLING TO BEAR. FREEDOM! *

THE PHILOSOPHER HERBERT MARCUSE & HIS FRIENDS JOIN A DEMONSTRATION MARCHING ON THE OAKLAND ARMY TERMINAL.

WHEN THEIR WAY IS BLOCKED BY A PHALANX OF RIOT POLICE, THE YOUNG DEMONSTRATORS SIT DOWN IN THE STREET & BURST INTO SONG.

* THESE ARE NOT THE ACTUAL LYRICS THEY WOULD HAVE SUNG — I WROTE THEM MYSELF JUST A COUPLE OF YEARS AGO, INSPIRED BY ALL I WAS LEARNING ABOUT HERBERT MARCUSE WHILE I WAS WRITING THIS COMIC.

CARTOONIST

PLEASURE

FREEDOM

EROS

RESISTANCE

IN 1965, MARCUSE COULD HAVE PASSED THROUGH THIS CROWD VIRTUALLY UNNOTICED.

WAIT A MINUTE— IS THAT— ?

One-Dimensional Man
HERBERT MARCUSE

BUT BY 1967, THE YOUNG REBELS IN THE PEACE & JUSTICE MOVEMENTS WERE TREATING HIM AS A ROCK STAR.

YES!

WHOOP!

MAESTRO!

A GROWNUP WHO GETS IT!

TODAY WE HAVE THE CAPACITY TO TURN THE WORLD INTO HELL, & WE ARE WELL ON OUR WAY TO DOING SO.

WE ALSO HAVE THE CAPACITY TO TURN IT INTO THE OPPOSITE OF HELL.

WHEN FRENCH WORKERS & STUDENTS WENT TO THE BARRICADES IN MAY 1968, THEIR SLOGANS REFLECTED MARCUSE'S IDEAS.

I BELIEVE THAT AS A RESULT OF THE ABOLITION OF POVERTY, MASSIVE WASTE, & THE DESTRUCTION OF RESOURCES—

—A WAY OF LIFE CAN BE FOUND IN WHICH HUMAN BEINGS TRULY DETERMINE THEIR EXISTENCE.

AND IN 1969, REFLECTING ON THE MAY 1968 UPRISING, MARCUSE WROTE:

ALL POWER—

—TO THE IMAGINATION

THIS "GREAT REFUSAL" RAISED A SPECTER: THE SPECTER OF SUBORDINATING PRODUCTIVE FORCES TO THE SOLIDARITY OF THE HUMAN SPECIES, ABOLISHING POVERTY & MISERY, THE ATTAINMENT OF PEACE.

THE YOUNG MILITANTS KNOW THAT WHAT IS AT STAKE IS THEIR OWN LIFE, WHICH HAS BECOME A PLAYTHING IN THE HANDS OF MANAGERS & GENERALS. THEY WANT TO TAKE IT OUT OF THESE HANDS & MAKE IT WORTH LIVING. AND THEY REALIZE THIS IS STILL POSSIBLE TODAY!

An Essay on Liberation
MARCUSE

CHAPTER 1

ASSIMILATION AND CATASTROPHE

A PHILOSOPHER ONCE FROM BERLIN—

THOUGHT ENJOYING LIFE WAS NO SIN.

HIS BODY HAS PASSED— GONE TO ASHES, ALAS— BUT HIS MEMORIES STAY WITH HIS KIN.

IN JULY 2003, A MEMORIAL FOR HERBERT MARCUSE WAS HELD IN BERLIN, GERMANY.

HIS SON, PETER MARCUSE, OFFERED SOME LIMERICKS TO MARK THE EVENT.

OK, I GOT A A FEW MORE.

WE'VE NOT COME HERE TO BURY MY FATHER. JUST HIS ASHES—SO WHY ALL THE BOTHER? THE ANSWER IS SIMPLE: HIS LIFE IS A SYMBOL. THE OCCASION WILL HELP MAKE IT MATTER.

DO WE REALLY WANT TO SAY KADDISH? FOR SOME OF US IT'S A MISH MASH OF CULTURE, RELIGION, AND A RATHER MOVING TRADITION. SO WHY NOT? AFTER ALL, HE WAS JEWISH.

GROAN

HA

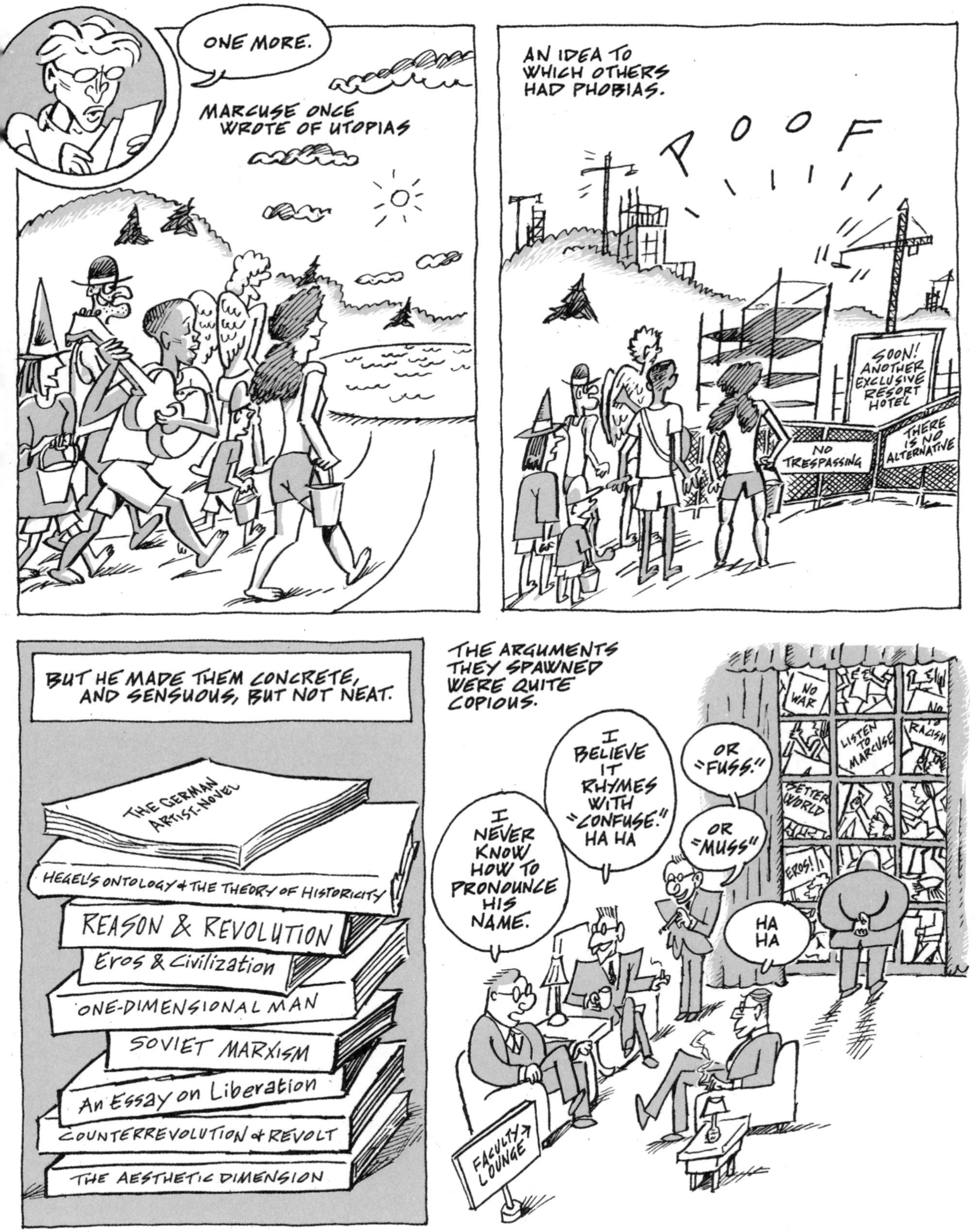
ONE MORE.
MARCUSE ONCE WROTE OF UTOPIAS
AN IDEA TO WHICH OTHERS HAD PHOBIAS.
POOF
SOON! ANOTHER EXCLUSIVE RESORT HOTEL
NO TRESPASSING
THERE IS NO ALTERNATIVE
BUT HE MADE THEM CONCRETE, AND SENSUOUS, BUT NOT NEAT.
THE GERMAN ARTIST-NOVEL
HEGEL'S ONTOLOGY & THE THEORY OF HISTORICITY
REASON & REVOLUTION
Eros & Civilization
ONE-DIMENSIONAL MAN
SOVIET MARXISM
An Essay on Liberation
COUNTERREVOLUTION & REVOLT
THE AESTHETIC DIMENSION
THE ARGUMENTS THEY SPAWNED WERE QUITE COPIOUS.
NO WAR
LISTEN TO MARCUSE
BETTER WORLD
EROS!
I NEVER KNOW HOW TO PRONOUNCE HIS NAME.
I BELIEVE IT RHYMES WITH "CONFUSE." HA HA
OR "FUSS."
OR "MUSS"
HA HA
FACULTY LOUNGE

HERBERT MARCUSE WAS BORN ON JULY 19, 1898, TO CARL & GERTRUD MARCUSE. CARL OWNED A FACTORY, AS DID GERTRUD'S FATHER.

THEY LIVED IN A NEIGHBORHOOD OF HIGHLY ASSIMILATED JEWISH FAMILIES.

HOW ASSIMILATED?

SIEGFRIED! BRUNHILDE! IT'S TIME TO COME INSIDE FOR SHABBAT!

SEE YA, HERBIE!

IN LATER YEARS MARCUSE REMEMBERED HEARING THIS CRY ON HIS STREET.

NIETZCHE
SCHILLER
SHAKESPEARE
ANDRÉ GIDE

HE READS ALL THE TIME. SHOULDN'T HE BE LEARNING THE BUSINESS?

LEAVE HIM BE. I NEVER HAD TIME TO READ WHEN I WAS A KID.

I'M NOT SURE I EVER EVEN WAS A KID.

Berliner Tageblatt

FOR MARCUSE, THE FERMENT OF IDEAS WAS INTERRUPTED BY THE FERMENT OF NATIONALISM, CLASS STRUGGLE, & **WAR**.

THE LAST THING I'LL STAND FOR IS IDEAS TO GET THE BETTER OF ME.

I SHOOT WITH LIVE AMMUNITION!

WHEN I HEAR THE WORD CULTURE, I RELEASE THE SAFETY ON MY BROWNING!

A VERSION OF THIS PHRASE IS OFTEN ATTRIBUTED TO JOSEF GOEBBELS BUT IT IS ACTUALLY FROM A NAZI PLAY.

WHEN WORLD WAR I BROKE OUT, MARCUSE WAS DRAFTED. CONSIGNED TO THE REAR ECHELON DUE TO POOR EYESIGHT, HE WOUND UP "WIPING HORSES' ASSES" FOR THE INFANTRY.

THE WAR WAS SUPPOSED TO LAST A FEW WEEKS, BUT DRAGGED ON FOR YEARS.

HERE'S TO WAR.

MY GOD HOW THE MONEY ROLLS IN!

SO YOU'RE UPSET ABOUT WAR PROFITEERING, THE ARROGANCE OF THE OFFICERS, & THE WHOLE IMPERIAL PROJECT THAT GOT US INTO THIS MESS.

YOU SHOULD JOIN OUR SOCIALIST MOVEMENT.

BUT DIDN'T THE SOCIALISTS VOTE FOR THE WAR?

WELL, YES, BUT EVERYBODY WANTED A WAR BACK THEN.

THE WAR WAS ALSO SUPPOSED TO NEUTRALIZE THE BURGEONING SOCIALIST SENTIMENT OF THE PRE-WAR YEARS.

INSTEAD—

FOR MILLIONS OF WORKING CLASS SOLDIERS ON ALL SIDES, IT REPLACED THE SLOW DEATH OF THE IMPOVERISHED WAGE EARNER WITH CERTAIN SLAUGHTER.

FORWARD MARCH!

WHY ARE YOU ALL BLEATING LIKE SHEEP?

BAAH! BAAAH! BAAAAH! BAAAH!

WE KNOW WE WON'T RETURN.

THE "SOCIAL-DEMOCRATIC" IDEAL OF GRADUAL CHANGE BEGAN TO GIVE WAY TO REVOLUTIONISM.

CHAPTER 2

THE SORROWS OF YOUNG MARCUSE

1918 REVOLUTION REPLACED THE GERMAN EMPIRE WITH A **REPUBLIC** LED BY THE SOCIAL DEMOCRATS (SPD), THE PARTY MARCUSE HAD JOINED DURING THE WAR. BUT AS SOON AS THEY TASTED POWER, THE SPD LEADERS TURNED THEIR ATTENTION TO COMFORTING THE COMFORTABLE AND AFFLICTING THE AFFLICTED.

NOT TO WORRY, HERR JUNKER, WE WILL NOT TAMPER WITH YOUR PREROGATIVES & PRIVILEGES.

WHAT TH'.?

AND ANY OF OUR CONSTITUENTS WHO OBJECTS WILL BE DEALT WITH SEVERELY!

1919 WHEN THE BERLIN WORKERS SAW THE SPD TURNING AGAINST THEM, THEY ROSE UP.

HOW DO I WORK THIS.?

AS A SOLDIERS' COUNCIL DELEGATE, MARCUSE WAS SENT TO THE BARRICADES TO DEFEND THE UPRISING. HIS ASSIGNMENT WAS TO RETURN THE FIRE OF RIGHT-WING MILITIAS (THE "FREIKORPS")

ROSA LUXEMBURG, AND OTHER PRINCIPLED SOCIALIST LEADERS WHO HAD BROKEN FROM THE SPD TO FORM THE SPARTACIST LEAGUE, JOINED THE REVOLT.

I SUPPOSE WE KNEW IT WAS HOPELESS.

BUT IN A TIME OF REVOLUTION, THE REVOLUTIONIST HAS NO CHOICE.

YOU CAN'T BE SELECTIVE IN THE COLLECTIVE.

FRÄULEIN LUXEMBURG!

YOU ARE UNDER ARREST!

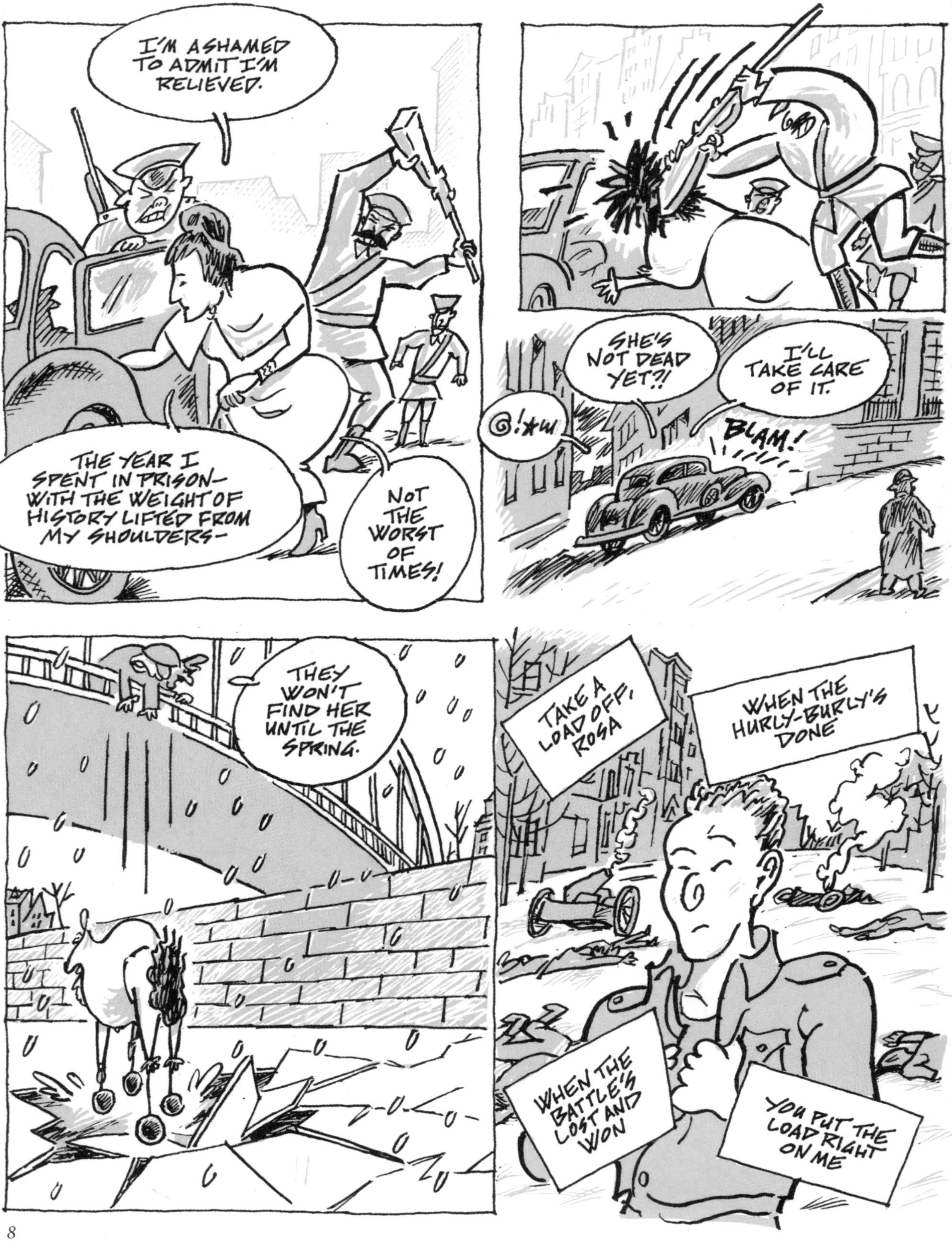
I'M ASHAMED TO ADMIT I'M RELIEVED.
THE YEAR I SPENT IN PRISON—WITH THE WEIGHT OF HISTORY LIFTED FROM MY SHOULDERS—
NOT THE WORST OF TIMES!
@!*W
SHE'S NOT DEAD YET?!
I'LL TAKE CARE OF IT.
BLAM!
THEY WON'T FIND HER UNTIL THE SPRING.
TAKE A LOAD OFF, ROSA
WHEN THE HURLY-BURLY'S DONE
WHEN THE BATTLE'S LOST AND WON
YOU PUT THE LOAD RIGHT ON ME

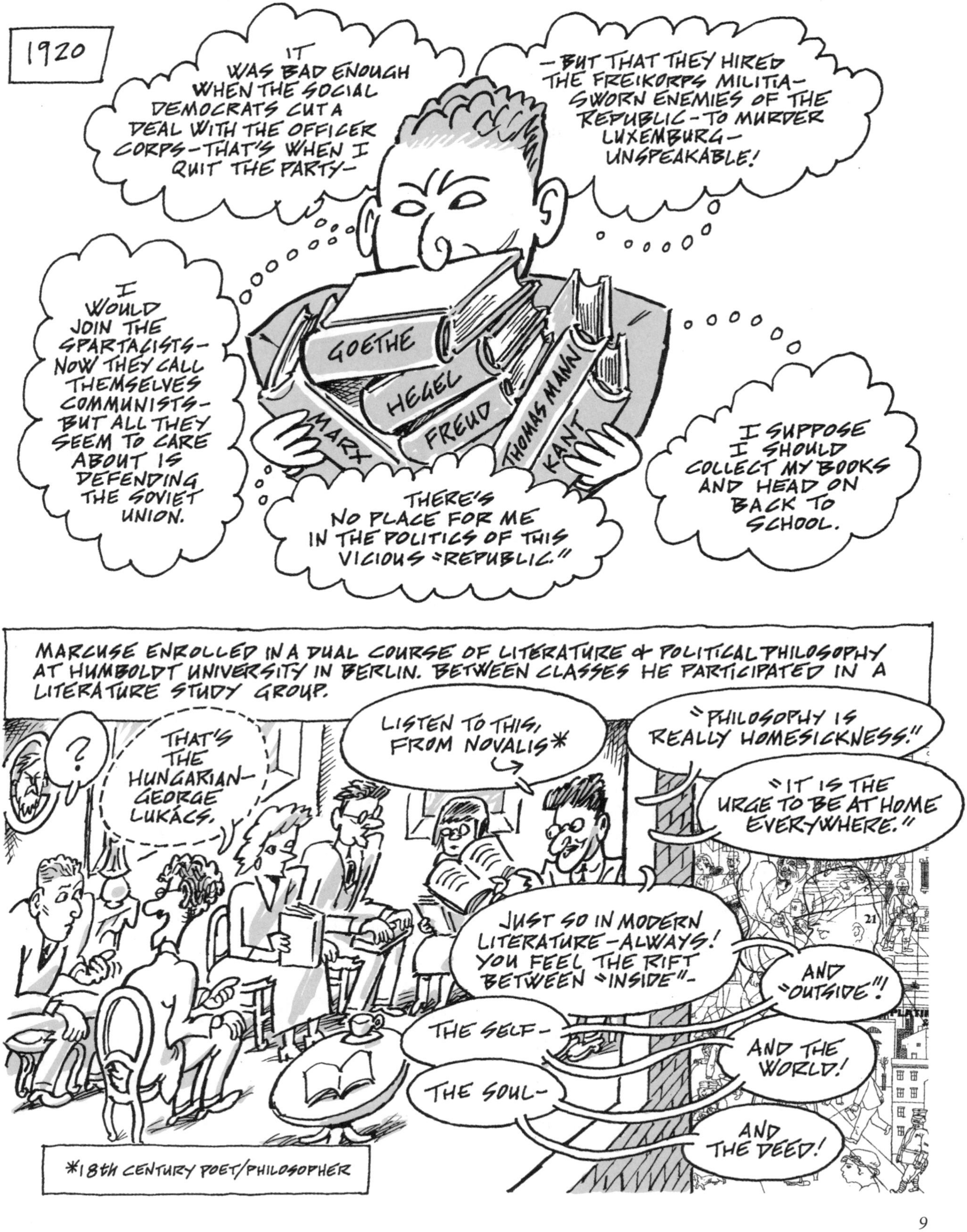

1920
IT WAS BAD ENOUGH WHEN THE SOCIAL DEMOCRATS CUT A DEAL WITH THE OFFICER CORPS—THAT'S WHEN I QUIT THE PARTY—
—BUT THAT THEY HIRED THE FREIKORPS MILITIA—SWORN ENEMIES OF THE REPUBLIC—TO MURDER LUXEMBURG—UNSPEAKABLE!
GOETHE
HEGEL
FREUD
MARX
THOMAS MANN
KANT
I WOULD JOIN THE SPARTACISTS—NOW THEY CALL THEMSELVES COMMUNISTS—BUT ALL THEY SEEM TO CARE ABOUT IS DEFENDING THE SOVIET UNION.
THERE'S NO PLACE FOR ME IN THE POLITICS OF THIS VICIOUS "REPUBLIC."
I SUPPOSE I SHOULD COLLECT MY BOOKS AND HEAD ON BACK TO SCHOOL.
MARCUSE ENROLLED IN A DUAL COURSE OF LITERATURE & POLITICAL PHILOSOPHY AT HUMBOLDT UNIVERSITY IN BERLIN. BETWEEN CLASSES HE PARTICIPATED IN A LITERATURE STUDY GROUP.
?
THAT'S THE HUNGARIAN—GEORGE LUKÁCS.
LISTEN TO THIS, FROM NOVALIS*
"PHILOSOPHY IS REALLY HOMESICKNESS."
"IT IS THE URGE TO BE AT HOME EVERYWHERE."
JUST SO IN MODERN LITERATURE—ALWAYS! YOU FEEL THE RIFT BETWEEN "INSIDE"—
AND "OUTSIDE"!
THE SELF—
AND THE WORLD!
THE SOUL—
AND THE DEED!
*18th CENTURY POET/PHILOSOPHER

THE LONGING TO ENGAGE WITH WHAT WAS "OUTSIDE"— A THWARTED & UNMOORED SOCIETY EMERGING IN THE WAKE OF MILITARY DEFEAT & STILLBORN REVOLUTION— ANIMATED YOUNG ARTISTS AS WELL AS BUDDING INTELLECTUALS.

GEORGE GROSZ, THE PRINTMAKER WHOSE X-RAY VIEW OF WEIMAR REPUBLIC VANITY AND DEPRAVITY APPEARS ON THE PREVIOUS PAGE, WAS PART OF THE

NEW OBJECTIVITY

MOVEMENT.

WHAT YOU SEE ON THESE CANVASES IS MY SOUL CRYING OUT.

YOUR TORTURED SOUL IS SUBLIME, I'M SURE.

MEANWHILE THE WORLD IS CRYING TOO!

THESE YOUNG ARTISTS— MOSTLY WWI VETS— REJECTED THE OTHER-WORLDLY EXPRESSIONISM OF AN OLDER GENERATION.

BERTOLT BRECHT & KURT WEILL'S THREEPENNY OPERA DRAMATIZED THE IDEA OF "GANGSTER CAPITALISM"—

WHAT IS THE ROBBING OF A BANK TO THE FOUNDING OF A BANK?

—WHILE OFFERING A GLIMPSE OF THE RAGE SIMMERING BELOW.

I'M COUNTING YOUR HEADS WHILE I MAKE UP THE BEDS!

IN FILM, G. W. PABST'S VERSION OF THREEPENNY ENDED WITH A CATHARTIC UPRISING MISSING IN THE ORIGINAL.

BUT FRITZ LANG'S "METROPOLIS" & "M" PAINTED A PESSIMISTIC PICTURE OF WHERE THE RAGE OF THE DOWNTRODDEN MIGHT LEAD.

AND F. W. MURNAU'S "THE LAST LAUGH" SATIRIZED (WITH COMPASSION) THE COMPLIANT WORKER'S ILLUSIONS.

"THE LAST LAUGH," WITH ITS SLUM-DWELLING HOTEL DOORMAN PUFFED UP BY THE ILLUSION OF STATUS THAT HIS UNIFORM CONFERS, COULD BE TAKEN AS AN ILLUSTRATION OF AN OFT-QUOTED REMARK OF MARCUSE'S:

WHEN I SAW THE ENLISTED MEN IN THE SOLDIERS' COUNCILS VOTING FOR THE VERY OFFICERS WHO HAD LED THEM TO SLAUGHTER DURING THE WAR—

I KNEW THE REVOLUTION WOULD FAIL.

SO IT WAS A DISAPPOINTED MARCUSE WHO BEGAN HIS INTELLECTUAL ADVENTURES EXPLORING THE ARTIST'S PROBLEM AS IF IT WERE THE PROBLEM OF REVOLUTION.

IN CASE OF DISAPPOINTMENT

BREAK GLASS

BLACK FOREST!

(BY THIS TIME MARCUSE HAD TRANSFERRED TO THE UNIVERSITY OF FREIBURG.)

IN HIS 1922 DISSERTATION, "THE GERMAN ARTIST-NOVEL," MARCUSE SAW

THE CLEFT BETWEEN WHAT IS & WHAT COULD BE

AS THE SOURCE AND THE SHAPE OF THE MODERN ARTIST'S DILEMMA:

THE VERY BEING OF AN ARTIST MEANS HAVING A PECULIAR TYPE OF LIFE, NOT CONGRUENT WITH THAT OF PEOPLE IN GENERAL.

WHICH MAKES IT DIFFICULT FOR THE ARTIST TO PRESENT A "FULL HISTORICAL PICTURE."

FOLLOWING LUKÁCS, MARCUSE CONTRASTED THE ISOLATION OF THE MODERN ARTIST WITH THE "EMBEDEDNESS" OF ARTISTS IN EARLIER TIMES.

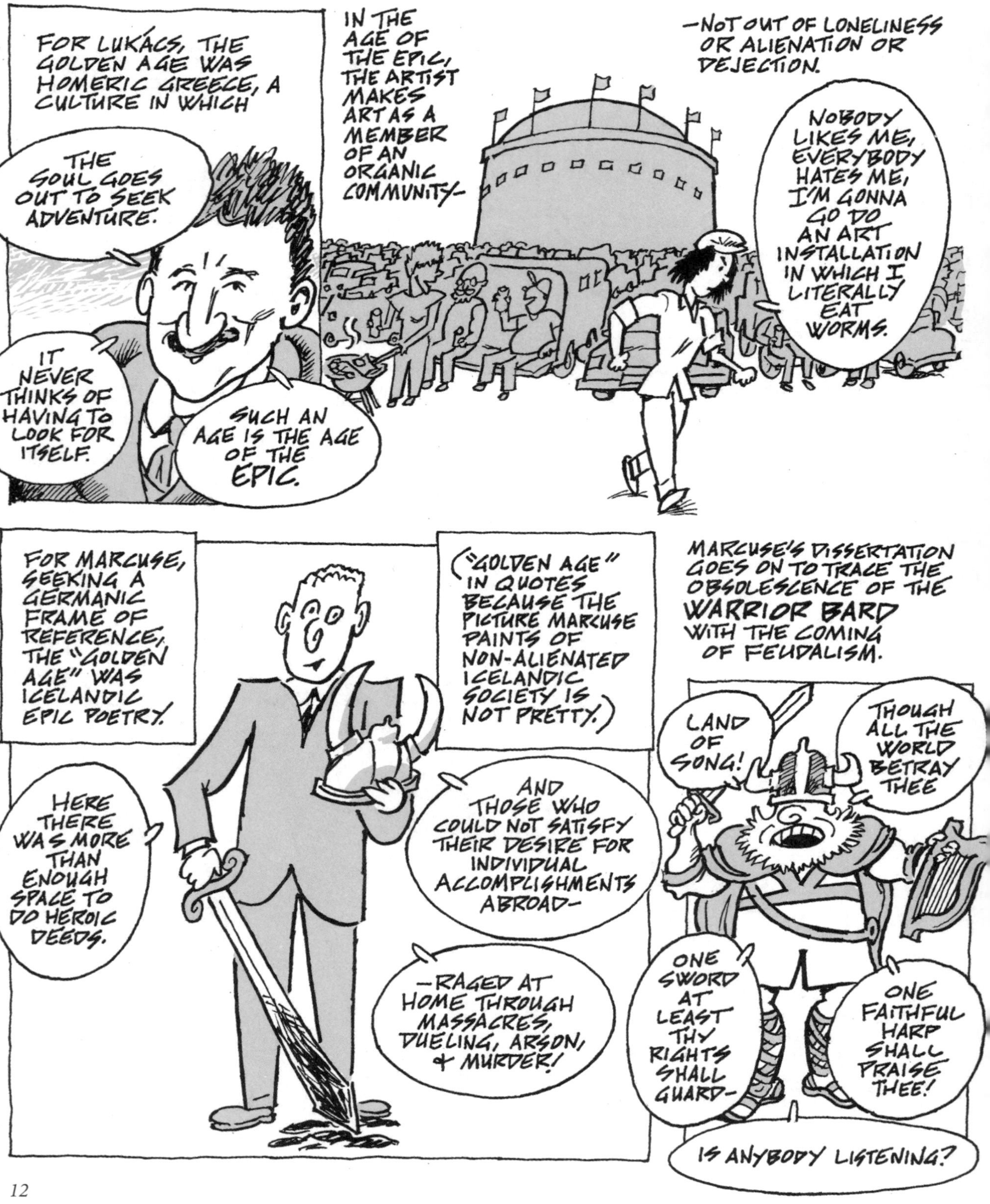
FOR LUKÁCS, THE GOLDEN AGE WAS HOMERIC GREECE, A CULTURE IN WHICH
THE SOUL GOES OUT TO SEEK ADVENTURE.
IT NEVER THINKS OF HAVING TO LOOK FOR ITSELF.
SUCH AN AGE IS THE AGE OF THE EPIC.
IN THE AGE OF THE EPIC, THE ARTIST MAKES ART AS A MEMBER OF AN ORGANIC COMMUNITY—
—NOT OUT OF LONELINESS OR ALIENATION OR DEJECTION.
NOBODY LIKES ME, EVERYBODY HATES ME, I'M GONNA GO DO AN ART INSTALLATION IN WHICH I LITERALLY EAT WORMS.
FOR MARCUSE, SEEKING A GERMANIC FRAME OF REFERENCE, THE "GOLDEN AGE" WAS ICELANDIC EPIC POETRY.
("GOLDEN AGE" IN QUOTES BECAUSE THE PICTURE MARCUSE PAINTS OF NON-ALIENATED ICELANDIC SOCIETY IS NOT PRETTY.)
HERE THERE WAS MORE THAN ENOUGH SPACE TO DO HEROIC DEEDS.
AND THOSE WHO COULD NOT SATISFY THEIR DESIRE FOR INDIVIDUAL ACCOMPLISHMENTS ABROAD—
—RAGED AT HOME THROUGH MASSACRES, DUELING, ARSON, & MURDER!
MARCUSE'S DISSERTATION GOES ON TO TRACE THE OBSOLESCENCE OF THE WARRIOR BARD WITH THE COMING OF FEUDALISM.
LAND OF SONG!
THOUGH ALL THE WORLD BETRAY THEE
ONE SWORD AT LEAST THY RIGHTS SHALL GUARD—
ONE FAITHFUL HARP SHALL PRAISE THEE!
IS ANYBODY LISTENING?

FEUDALISM REPLACED THE BARD WITH A FAMILIAR ARTIST TROPE, THE **VAGABOND.**

AS SOON AS EARTHLY LIFE WAS STRIPPED OF THE GODS—

—THE SPIRIT HAD TO PRESENT ITSELF PURELY AS UNTETHERED TO REALITY—AND IN OPPOSITION TO IT.

TRAVELING BANDS OF MUSICIANS AND MIMES AND, ESPECIALLY, YOUNG CLERICS AND STUDENTS, BROKE FREE AND CHARGED OUT INTO A LIFE OF LAUGHTER.

TOO PROUD, TOO WILD TO EVER SEEK COMPROMISE OR STABILITY—

—THEIR LIVES EVAPORATED INTO AUSTERE BEGGING AND CONTINUAL WANDERING.

HA HA HA HA HA HA HA HA HA HA HA

FURTHER

MOAN GROAN

POEMS 5¢ EACH

WHICH BRINGS US TO MODERNITY, AND THE GERMAN ARTIST-NOVEL, A LITERARY FORM WHICH MARCUSE'S DISSERTATION TRACES FROM THE 17th CENTURY TO THE 20th.

"I TREAT MY HEART LIKE A SICK CHILD AND GRATIFY ITS EVERY FANCY."

"THE HUMAN RACE IS A MONOTONOUS AFFAIR."

OH GET OVER YOURSELF.

GOETHE
The Sorrows of Young Werther

MARCUSE SEES THE RENUNCIATION OF PROSAIC SOCIETY IN GOETHE'S 1774 NOVEL AS ESCAPIST & NARROW.

INBORN IN NEARLY EVERY ARTIST'S NATURE IS A VOLUPTUOUS, TREACHEROUS TENDENCY TO ACCEPT INJUSTICE IF IT CREATES BEAUTY.

WOW!!

DEATH IN VENICE BY THOMAS MANN

HE PREFERS THE MORE WORLDLY AND "EPIC" CONCERNS OF GOETHE'S LATER WORK, AND OF THOMAS MANN'S CELEBRATED 1912 NOVELLA.

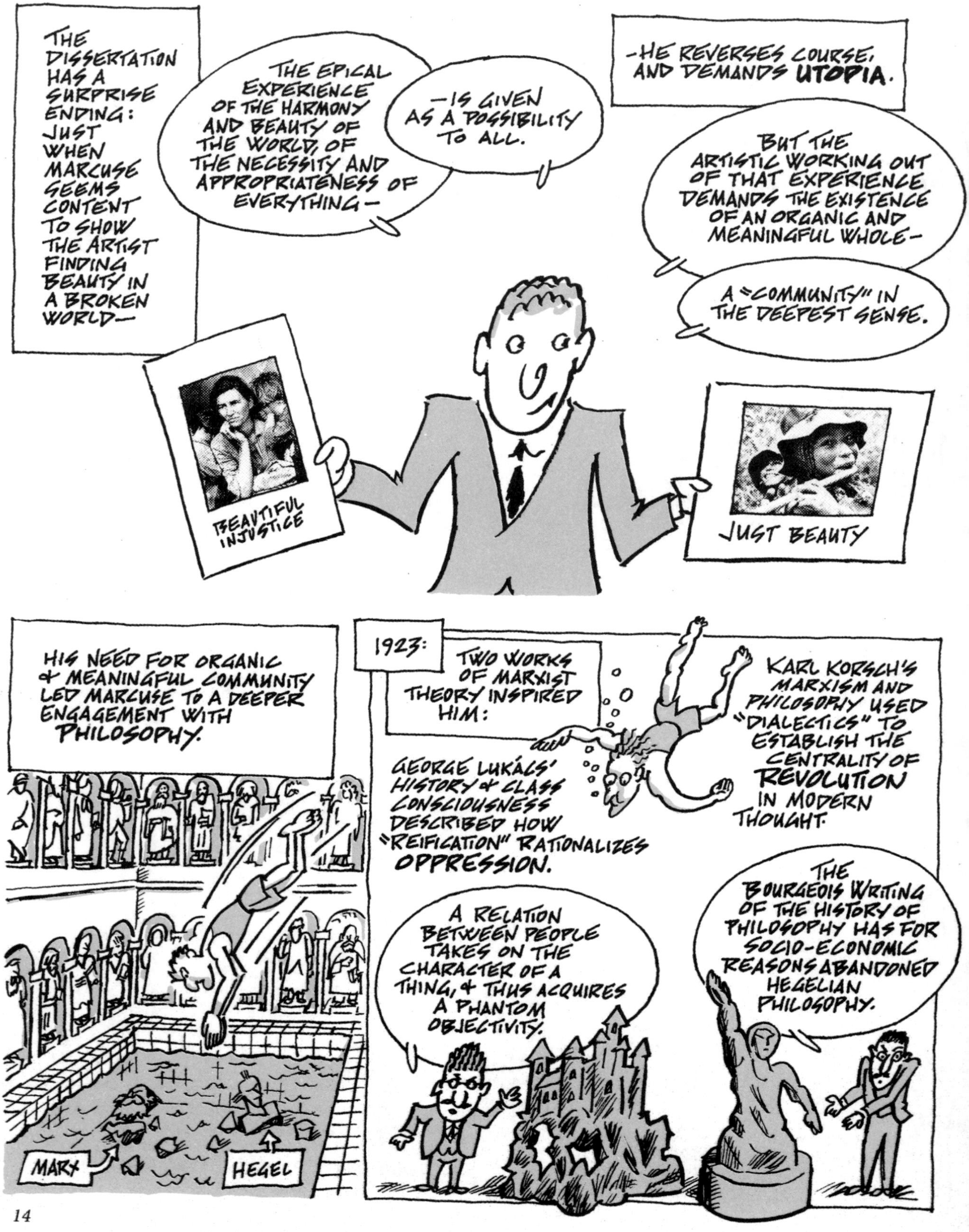
THE DISSERTATION HAS A SURPRISE ENDING: JUST WHEN MARCUSE SEEMS CONTENT TO SHOW THE ARTIST FINDING BEAUTY IN A BROKEN WORLD—
THE EPICAL EXPERIENCE OF THE HARMONY AND BEAUTY OF THE WORLD, OF THE NECESSITY AND APPROPRIATENESS OF EVERYTHING—
—IS GIVEN AS A POSSIBILITY TO ALL.
—HE REVERSES COURSE, AND DEMANDS UTOPIA.
BUT THE ARTISTIC WORKING OUT OF THAT EXPERIENCE DEMANDS THE EXISTENCE OF AN ORGANIC AND MEANINGFUL WHOLE—
A "COMMUNITY" IN THE DEEPEST SENSE.
BEAUTIFUL INJUSTICE
JUST BEAUTY
HIS NEED FOR ORGANIC & MEANINGFUL COMMUNITY LED MARCUSE TO A DEEPER ENGAGEMENT WITH PHILOSOPHY.
MARX
HEGEL
1923:
TWO WORKS OF MARXIST THEORY INSPIRED HIM:
GEORGE LUKÁCS' HISTORY & CLASS CONSCIOUSNESS DESCRIBED HOW "REIFICATION" RATIONALIZES OPPRESSION.
KARL KORSCH'S MARXISM AND PHILOSOPHY USED "DIALECTICS" TO ESTABLISH THE CENTRALITY OF REVOLUTION IN MODERN THOUGHT.
A RELATION BETWEEN PEOPLE TAKES ON THE CHARACTER OF A THING, & THUS ACQUIRES A PHANTOM OBJECTIVITY.
THE BOURGEOIS WRITING OF THE HISTORY OF PHILOSOPHY HAS FOR SOCIO-ECONOMIC REASONS ABANDONED HEGELIAN PHILOSOPHY.

PHILOSOPHY, POETRY, & CRITICISM BECAME THE THREE CORNERS OF

The Triangle

—A SHORT-LIVED EXPERIMENTAL MONTHLY THAT MARCUSE WORKED ON AFTER HE RETURNED TO BERLIN.

PHILOSOPHY POETRY AND CRITICISM

ARE DESCRIBED IN THIS JOURNAL AS THE "THREE STAGES OF THE RETROGRADE MARCH OF THE SPIRIT TOWARDS INTELLECT."

MARCUSE'S OWN MARCH OF THE SPIRIT TOWARDS INTELLECT—RETROGRADE OR NOT—TOOK HIM THROUGH THE RICHES OF WEIMAR REPUBLIC CULTURE.

1924:

MARRIED SOPHIE WERTHEIM, A MATHEMATICIAN HE MET IN FREIBURG.

THEY SET UP HOUSEKEEPING ON A LOWER FLOOR OF HIS FATHER'S APARTMENT BUILDING IN BERLIN.

ARISE!

WHO WANTS TO HELP ME STUFF ENVELOPES?

THEIR APARTMENT BECAME A KIND OF SALON WHERE ARTISTS, SCHOLARS, & ACTIVISTS DISCUSSED MARXISM, PSYCHOLOGY, THEATER, & PAINTING. A FREQUENT VISITOR WAS HERBERT'S YOUNGER BROTHER ERICH (THE MORE POLITICALLY ACTIVE MARCUSE AT THIS TIME).

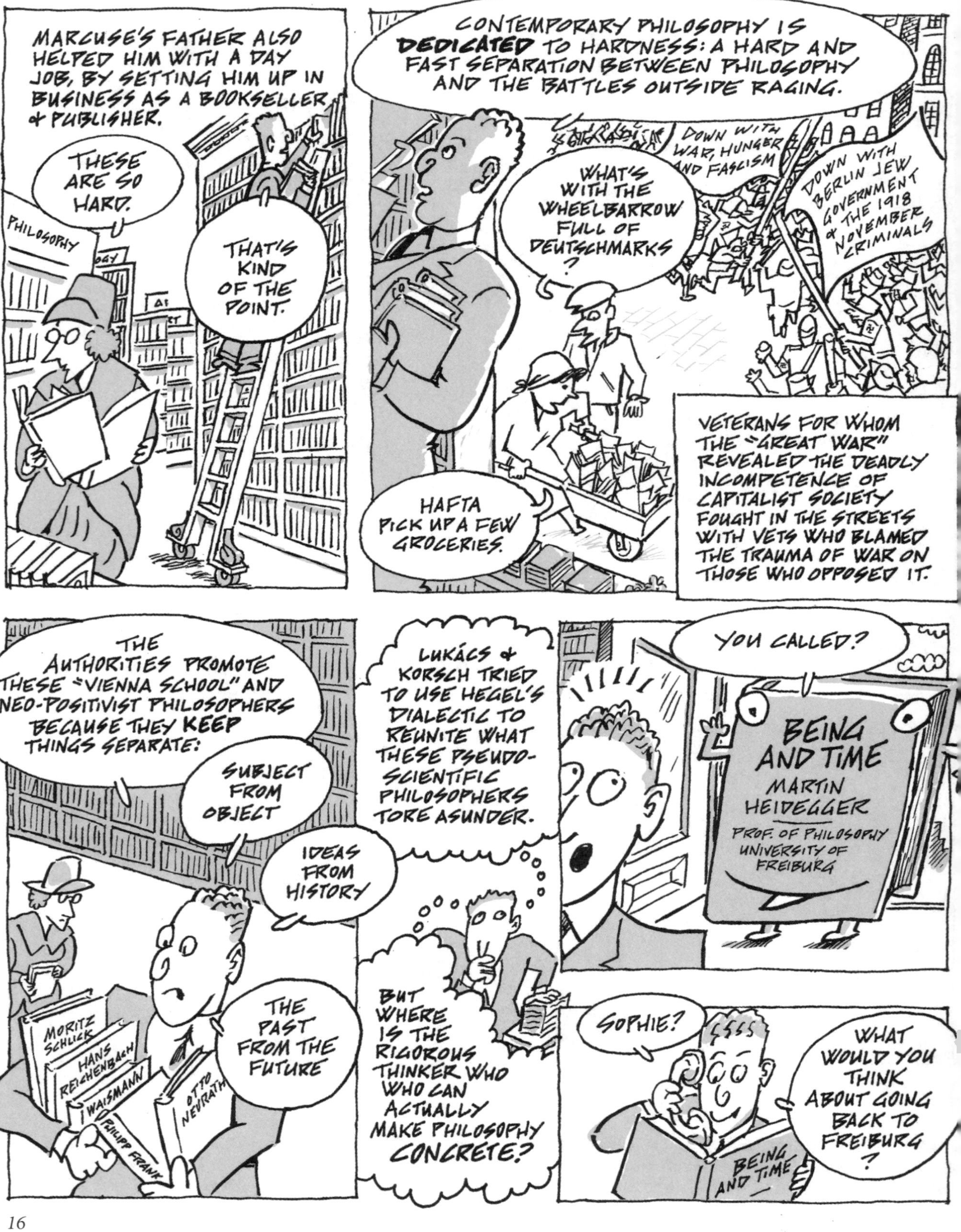
MARCUSE'S FATHER ALSO HELPED HIM WITH A DAY JOB, BY SETTING HIM UP IN BUSINESS AS A BOOKSELLER & PUBLISHER.
THESE ARE SO HARD.
PHILOSOPHY
THAT'S KIND OF THE POINT.
CONTEMPORARY PHILOSOPHY IS DEDICATED TO HARDNESS: A HARD AND FAST SEPARATION BETWEEN PHILOSOPHY AND THE BATTLES OUTSIDE RAGING.
DOWN WITH WAR, HUNGER AND FASCISM
DOWN WITH BERLIN JEW GOVERNMENT & THE 1918 NOVEMBER CRIMINALS
WHAT'S WITH THE WHEELBARROW FULL OF DEUTSCHMARKS?
HAFTA PICK UP A FEW GROCERIES.
VETERANS FOR WHOM THE "GREAT WAR" REVEALED THE DEADLY INCOMPETENCE OF CAPITALIST SOCIETY FOUGHT IN THE STREETS WITH VETS WHO BLAMED THE TRAUMA OF WAR ON THOSE WHO OPPOSED IT.
THE AUTHORITIES PROMOTE THESE "VIENNA SCHOOL" AND NEO-POSITIVIST PHILOSOPHERS BECAUSE THEY KEEP THINGS SEPARATE:
SUBJECT FROM OBJECT
IDEAS FROM HISTORY
THE PAST FROM THE FUTURE
MORITZ SCHLICK
HANS REICHENBACH
WAISMANN
OTTO NEURATH
PHILIPP FRANK
LUKÁCS & KORSCH TRIED TO USE HEGEL'S DIALECTIC TO REUNITE WHAT THESE PSEUDO-SCIENTIFIC PHILOSOPHERS TORE ASUNDER.
BUT WHERE IS THE RIGOROUS THINKER WHO WHO CAN ACTUALLY MAKE PHILOSOPHY CONCRETE?
YOU CALLED?
BEING AND TIME
MARTIN HEIDEGGER
PROF. OF PHILOSOPHY UNIVERSITY OF FREIBURG
SOPHIE?
WHAT WOULD YOU THINK ABOUT GOING BACK TO FREIBURG?
BEING AND TIME

CHAPTER 3

FASCISTS AND FRANKFURTERS

1928

RESOLUTENESS IS NOT A WAY OF ESCAPE!

WANTING TO HAVE CONSCIENCE DOES NOT SIGNIFY A KIND OF SECLUSION!

IT BRINGS ONE, WITHOUT ILLUSIONS, INTO THE RESOLUTENESS OF TAKING ACTION!

MARTIN HEIDEGGER WAS A PHILOSOPHY SUPERSTAR WHEN MARCUSE BECAME HIS STUDENT & ASSISTANT IN FREIBURG.

HANNAH ARENDT

MARCUSE DESCRIBED THE SCENE IN A LETTER TO A FRIEND IN BERLIN:

Heidegger lectures in an overflowing auditorium, in brilliant lectures with unshakeable certainty, with that pleasant tremor in his voice, in a sports outfit like a chauffeur's uniform, with the pathos of a teacher who feels himself to be a prophet and pathfinder, and whom one indeed believes to be so.

WHAT MADE HEIDEGGER A "PATH-FINDER" FOR A YOUNG SOCIALIST LIKE MARCUSE?

BLACK FOREST

IN LATER YEARS MARCUSE SAID:

IT SEEMED TO US THAT HEIDEGGER OFFERED US A CHANCE TO LEAP ACROSS A GREAT DIVIDE.

BERLIN

HEIDEGGER OFFERED AN ALTERNATIVE:

THE GREAT DIVIDE:

NEVER MIND

NO HARM DONE

DESPITE WAR & REPRESSION, ESTABLISHED PHILOSOPHY (& ORTHODOX MARXISM) CLUNG TO A DETERMINISTIC FAITH IN SCIENCE & PROGRESS.

A VIEW OF THE WORLD THAT STRESSED THE SUBJECTIVITY & AUTHENTICITY—IMPLICITLY, THE FREEDOM—OF THE INDIVIDUAL.

THE WORLD OF PHILOSOPHY IS A SERIES OF CONVERSATIONS, SOMETIMES BETWEEN THE LIVING & THE DEAD.

LET ME WARM YOU WITH THE BLAZE OF MY TOWERING INTELLECT!

LÖWITH

MARCUSE

ARENDT

JONAS

HEIDEGGER SEEMED TO BE A MAGNET FOR BRIGHT JEWISH STUDENTS.

HIS LENGTHY AFFAIR WITH HANNAH ARENDT IS LEGENDARY.

I'VE BEEN OFFERED A PRESTIGIOUS POST AT HUMBOLDT UNIVERSITY IN BERLIN, HANNAH.

BUT I WILL REMAIN AT FREIBURG, CLOSE TO MY BELOVED MOUNTAIN COTTAGE.

MY WORK IS **INTIMATELY ROOTED** IN THE LIVES OF THESE PEASANTS!

DOES THAT MEAN WE HAVE TO HAVE DINNER WITH THE PEASANTS AGAIN?

HEIDEGGER'S SENTIMENTAL ENTHUSIASM FOR FORESTS & MOUNTAINS & TOILING FARMERS MAY HAVE BEEN ONE REASON MARCUSE LOST CONFIDENCE IN HIS MENTOR. IN ANY EVENT—

WOOF! WOOF!

Contributions to a Phenomenology of Historical Materialism

HERBERT MARCUSE

—MARCUSE'S FIRST PUBLISHED ARTICLE DREW ON HISTORICAL MATERIALISM (MARXISM) & THE MEMORY OF URBAN STRUGGLE TO OFFER A CAUTIOUS CRITIQUE OF HEIDEGGER'S IDEAS.

IN THIS ESSAY MARCUSE, LIKE HEIDEGGER, REJECTS THE POSITIVISTS' ASSUMPTION THAT A PERSON WORDLESSLY ENCOUNTERS A REALITY STANDING **OVER** & **ABOVE** HIM/HER-SELF.—

—AND HE EMBRACES HEIDEGGER'S IDEA OF "HISTORICITY"—

—THE PAST THAT WE USE, THAT MOVES US.

BUT HE SPOTS A PROBLEM: WHAT INTERESTS HEIDEGGER IS NOT THE **AIMS** OF THE REBEL—

I DESPISE THE AGITATION & THE IDLE CHATTER OF THE DAY.

YAWN!

FAP!

—BUT ONLY THE **STANCE** OF REBELLION ITSELF.

WHEREAS, REALLY, THE **RADICAL ACT** SHOULD LIBERATE A NEW AND **NECESSARY** REALITY!

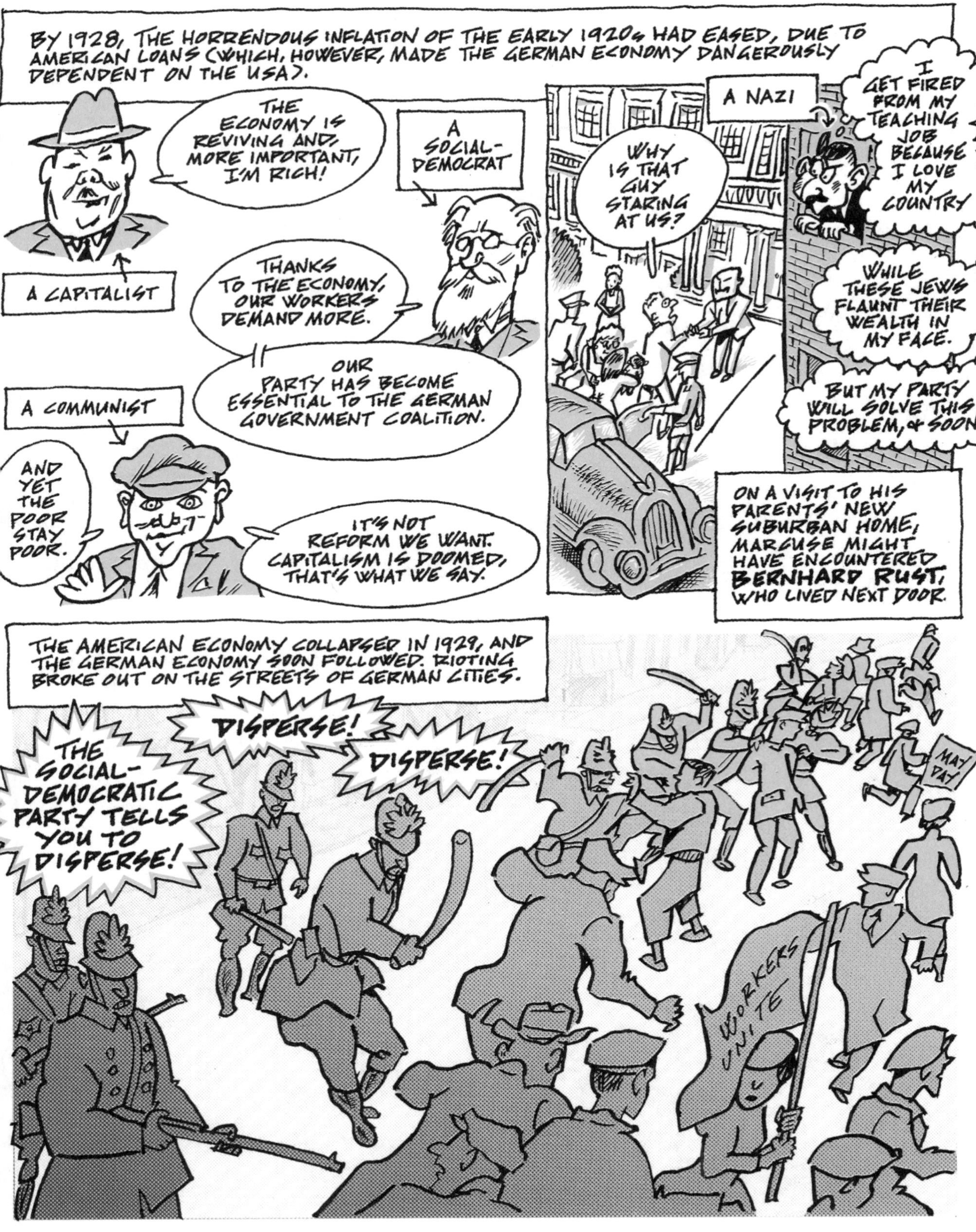
BY 1928, THE HORRENDOUS INFLATION OF THE EARLY 1920s HAD EASED, DUE TO AMERICAN LOANS (WHICH, HOWEVER, MADE THE GERMAN ECONOMY DANGEROUSLY DEPENDENT ON THE USA).
THE ECONOMY IS REVIVING AND, MORE IMPORTANT, I'M RICH!
A CAPITALIST
A SOCIAL-DEMOCRAT
THANKS TO THE ECONOMY, OUR WORKERS DEMAND MORE.
OUR PARTY HAS BECOME ESSENTIAL TO THE GERMAN GOVERNMENT COALITION.
A COMMUNIST
AND YET THE POOR STAY POOR.
IT'S NOT REFORM WE WANT. CAPITALISM IS DOOMED, THAT'S WHAT WE SAY.
A NAZI
WHY IS THAT GUY STARING AT US?
I GET FIRED FROM MY TEACHING JOB BECAUSE I LOVE MY COUNTRY
WHILE THESE JEWS FLAUNT THEIR WEALTH IN MY FACE.
BUT MY PARTY WILL SOLVE THIS PROBLEM, & SOON!
ON A VISIT TO HIS PARENTS' NEW SUBURBAN HOME, MARCUSE MIGHT HAVE ENCOUNTERED BERNHARD RUST, WHO LIVED NEXT DOOR.
THE AMERICAN ECONOMY COLLAPSED IN 1929, AND THE GERMAN ECONOMY SOON FOLLOWED. RIOTING BROKE OUT ON THE STREETS OF GERMAN CITIES.
THE SOCIAL-DEMOCRATIC PARTY TELLS YOU TO DISPERSE!
DISPERSE!
DISPERSE!
MAY DAY
WORKERS UNITE

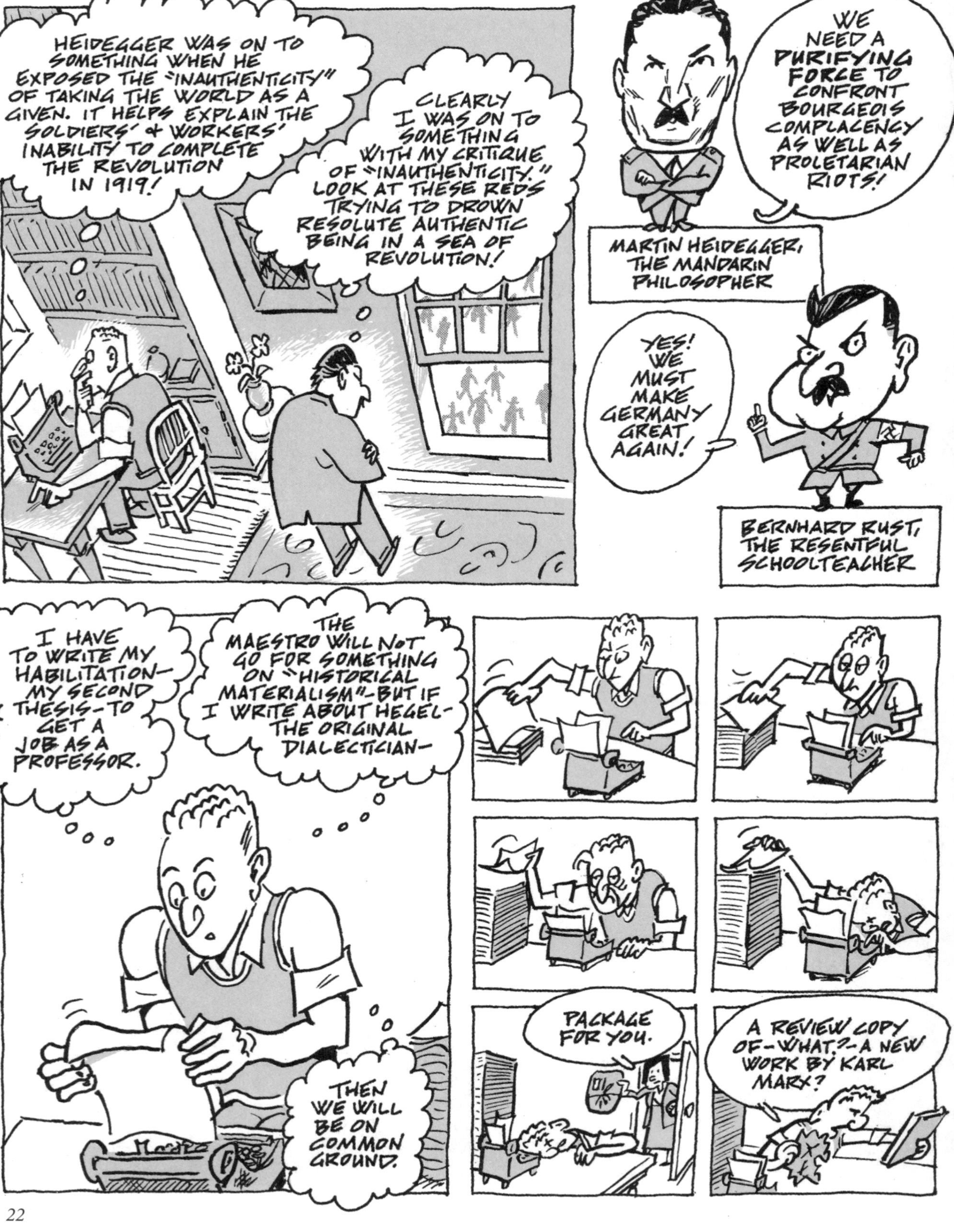

HEIDEGGER WAS ON TO SOMETHING WHEN HE EXPOSED THE "INAUTHENTICITY" OF TAKING THE WORLD AS A GIVEN. IT HELPS EXPLAIN THE SOLDIERS' & WORKERS' INABILITY TO COMPLETE THE REVOLUTION IN 1919!
CLEARLY I WAS ON TO SOMETHING WITH MY CRITIQUE OF "INAUTHENTICITY." LOOK AT THESE REDS TRYING TO DROWN RESOLUTE AUTHENTIC BEING IN A SEA OF REVOLUTION!
WE NEED A PURIFYING FORCE TO CONFRONT BOURGEOIS COMPLACENCY AS WELL AS PROLETARIAN RIOTS!
MARTIN HEIDEGGER, THE MANDARIN PHILOSOPHER
YES! WE MUST MAKE GERMANY GREAT AGAIN!
BERNHARD RUST, THE RESENTFUL SCHOOLTEACHER
I HAVE TO WRITE MY HABILITATION— MY SECOND THESIS—TO GET A JOB AS A PROFESSOR.
THE MAESTRO WILL NOT GO FOR SOMETHING ON "HISTORICAL MATERIALISM"—BUT IF I WRITE ABOUT HEGEL— THE ORIGINAL DIALECTICIAN—
THEN WE WILL BE ON COMMON GROUND.
PACKAGE FOR YOU.
A REVIEW COPY OF—WHAT?—A NEW WORK BY KARL MARX?

K·MARX — THE ECONOMIC & PHILOSOPHICAL MANUSCRIPTS OF 1844

WAS NOT NEW, OF COURSE, BUT IT WAS NEWLY DISCOVERED.

THESE MANUSCRIPTS USE ECONOMICS TO DEMYSTIFY HEGEL—

—AND HEGEL TO RESTORE OUR HUMANITY TO ECONOMICS!

MARCUSE WAS ONE OF THE FIRST TO REVIEW IT.

HERE ARE SOME OF MARCUSE'S FINDINGS, BEGINNING WITH SOMETHING HE LEARNED FROM THE PUBLISHER'S PREFACE:

WHEN MARX BEGAN THESE MANUSCRIPTS, HE DIVIDED A SHEET INTO THREE COLUMNS—

WAGES PROFITS RENTS

—BUT SOON FOUND HIMSELF WRITING ACROSS THE COLUMNS, FINALLY REPLACING HIS THREE HEADS WITH ONE:

Estranged Labor

ESTRANGEMENT, THE REDUCTION OF ALL THE WORLD'S POSSIBILITIES TO NARROW CATEGORIES OF POTENTIAL GAIN, CREATES (IN MARCUSE'S PARAPHRASE)

AN ALIEN WORLD THAT CONFRONTS US AS A HOSTILE POWER.

DON'T CALL US, WE'LL CALL YOU.

IF YOU'RE SO SMART, WHY AREN'T YOU RICH?

IT'S NOT WHAT YOU KNOW, IT'S WHO YOU KNOW.

DON'T SELL THE STEAK, SELL THE SIZZLE.

SUCK IT UP.

THAT'S HOW THE WORLD LOOKS TO US— HOW DO WE LOOK TO THE WORLD?

A HUMAN BEING IS REDUCED IN CAPITALISM TO AN ACTIVITY AND A BELLY.

LATER, MARCUSE WOULD RECALL THAT AFTER THE 1844 MANUSCRIPTS APPEARED,

HEIDEGGER VS. MARX WAS NO LONGER A PROBLEM FOR ME.

MARCUSE'S "HABILITATION" WAS PUBLISHED UNDER THE TITLE HEGEL'S ONTOLOGY & THE THEORY OF HISTORICITY. HIS WHOLE FAMILY CAME TO FRIEBURG TO CELEBRATE.

BUT IN 1932—

LOOK, PETER, YOUR DADDY WROTE A BOOK!

DO YOU THINK PROFESSOR HEIDEGGER WILL LIKE IT?

NOW I AM SOMEBODY!

BOOK BY ME

HEGEL'S ONTOLOGY, MARCUSE'S FIRST BOOK, NEVER MENTIONS MARX.

BUT IT DOES GRAPPLE WITH "ESTRANGEMENT" BY ASKING HOW **BIFURCATION** THWARTS UNDERSTANDING.

THE "THEORY OF HISTORICITY" IS FLESHED OUT WITH SPECIFICS: LABOR, DEPENDENCE, **COLLECTIVE MEMORY.**

SOUL

BODY

SUBJECT

OBJECT

SELF

WORLD

BEING

NOT BEING

WHEN OPPOSITES LOSE THEIR LIVING RELATION WITH EACH OTHER & BECOME SELF-CONTAINED, THE NEED FOR PHILOSOPHY ARISES.

BECAUSE LIFE IS AT ONCE **SUBJECT** & **PREDICATE!**

HEGEL

WE → REVOLUTION

MADE

THE PLUTOCRATS → RULE

LET THE SPD

SPD RULE → UNREST

DID NOT STOP

WILL THE PLUTOCRATS → RULE?

LET THE NAZIS

MAYBE WE WERE WRONG TO SNEER AT THE NAZIS.

THEY **TALK** ABOUT FIGHTING THE BOURGEOISIE—

BUT WHAT THEY'RE **GOOD** AT IS BEATING UP **REDS** & **JEWS!**

PLUTOCRATS

(HERE'S THE 2016 VERSION.)

HE **TALKS** ABOUT BRINGING JOBS BACK.

PROTECTIONISM!

BUILD THE WALL

MAKE AMERI GR8 AGAIN

BUT HE **REALLY** JUST WANTS TO RELIEVE US OF OUR **REGULATORY BURDEN!**

AS 1932 DREW TO A CLOSE—

OUR PARTY IS POISED TO WIN THE ELECTION! SOON WE WILL CLEANSE OUR SCHOOLS OF ALL DECADENT NON-ARYAN INFLUENCE!＊

I'M GLAD YOU LIKE MY BOOK, PROFESSOR HUSSERL.

BUT IT'S USELESS TO SUBMIT IT TO HEIDEGGER.

NO ACADEMIC JOBS IN GERMANY FOR ME!

HEGEL'S ONTOLOGY OF THE THEORY

MAYBE THERE'S SOMETHING I CAN DO.

＊WHEN HITLER CAME TO POWER, BERNHARD RUST (SEE P. 23) WAS MADE MINISTER OF SCIENCE, EDUCATION, & NATIONAL CULTURE.

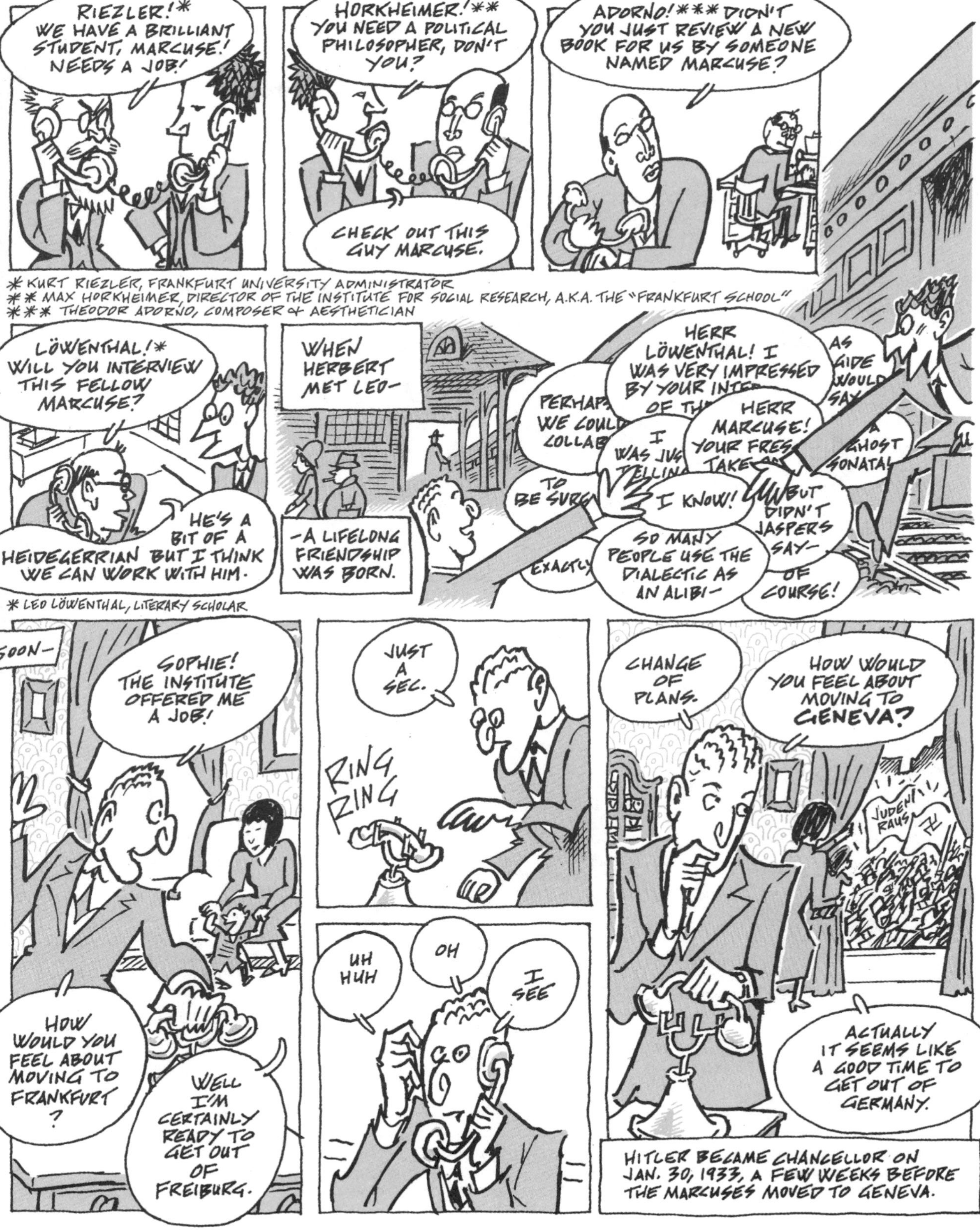
RIEZLER!* WE HAVE A BRILLIANT STUDENT, MARCUSE! NEEDS A JOB!
HORKHEIMER!** YOU NEED A POLITICAL PHILOSOPHER, DON'T YOU?
CHECK OUT THIS GUY MARCUSE.
ADORNO!*** DIDN'T YOU JUST REVIEW A NEW BOOK FOR US BY SOMEONE NAMED MARCUSE?
* KURT RIEZLER, FRANKFURT UNIVERSITY ADMINISTRATOR
** MAX HORKHEIMER, DIRECTOR OF THE INSTITUTE FOR SOCIAL RESEARCH, A.K.A. THE "FRANKFURT SCHOOL"
*** THEODOR ADORNO, COMPOSER & AESTHETICIAN
LÖWENTHAL!* WILL YOU INTERVIEW THIS FELLOW MARCUSE?
HE'S A BIT OF A HEIDEGERRIAN BUT I THINK WE CAN WORK WITH HIM.
* LEO LÖWENTHAL, LITERARY SCHOLAR
WHEN HERBERT MET LEO—
HERR LÖWENTHAL! I WAS VERY IMPRESSED BY YOUR
HERR MARCUSE! YOUR
I KNOW!
BUT DIDN'T JASPERS SAY—
SO MANY PEOPLE USE THE DIALECTIC AS AN ALIBI—
OF COURSE!
—A LIFELONG FRIENDSHIP WAS BORN.
SOON—
SOPHIE! THE INSTITUTE OFFERED ME A JOB!
HOW WOULD YOU FEEL ABOUT MOVING TO FRANKFURT?
WELL I'M CERTAINLY READY TO GET OUT OF FREIBURG.
JUST A SEC.
RING RING
UH HUH
OH
I SEE
CHANGE OF PLANS.
HOW WOULD YOU FEEL ABOUT MOVING TO GENEVA?
JUDEN RAUS
ACTUALLY IT SEEMS LIKE A GOOD TIME TO GET OUT OF GERMANY.
HITLER BECAME CHANCELLOR ON JAN. 30, 1933, A FEW WEEKS BEFORE THE MARCUSES MOVED TO GENEVA.

WHAT WAS THE FRANKFURT SCHOOL?
(AND WHAT WERE THEY DOING IN GENEVA IN 1933?)

THE INSTITUTE FOR SOCIAL RESEARCH WAS THE BRAINCHILD OF FELIX WEIL, LIKE MARCUSE A VETERAN OF THE 1919 UPRISING.

1923

YES, FELIX, YOU WILL GET YOUR INSTITUTE.

WE ARE **OPTIMISTS** IN THE MIDST OF **RUINS.** WE SEE THE TRANSITION TO SOCIALISM **ADVANCING RELENTLESSLY!**

CARL GRÜNBERG, INSTITUTE DIRECTOR DURING THE 1920s

AND WE INTEND TO **SUPPORT** THIS TRANSITION WITH **RIGOROUS EMPIRICAL RESEARCH.**

THE MARX-LENIN INSTITUTE IN MOSCOW IS OUR FRIEND, BUT NOT OUR **BOSS.**

IT WAS ENDOWED BY FELIX'S FATHER, A WEALTHY GRAIN MERCHANT.

THE INSTITUTE'S STUDENTS INCLUDED HANS GERTH, PAUL BARAN, & OSCAR H. SWEDE, WHO WROTE TO HIS AMERICAN FRIEND MAX EASTMAN IN 1927: ✳

GOD! THE HOURS I'VE SPENT LISTENING TO STRAW-SPLITTING SEMINARIANS CONVINCED THAT RELATIVITY IS **BOURGEOIS IDEOLOGY** TRYING TO TEAR DOWN NEWTON'S MATERIALISM—

AND **GRÜNBERG!** PREACHING THAT WE MAY SIT WITH ARMS FOLDED & WAIT FOR THE MILLENNIUM TO BLOSSOM FROM THE DUNG OF CAPITALIST DECAY!

BUT DETERMINISM CANNOT CREATE EITHER FIGHTING OR CREATIVE FORCES!

1930

I'M NOT WELL ENOUGH TO LEAD THE INSTITUTE ANY MORE, HORKHEIMER. YOU'LL HAVE TO TAKE OVER.

IS IT OK THAT I'M NOT EXACTLY AN OPTIMIST?

✳ HANS GERTH WAS MY PROFESSOR, & SUBSEQUENTLY MY COUSIN'S FATHER-IN-LAW, AT THE U. OF WISCONSIN IN THE 1960s. BARAN BECAME A MAINSTAY OF *MONTHLY REVIEW*, AN AMERICAN MARXIST ECONOMICS JOURNAL. OSCAR SWEDE WOUND UP IN LONDON, WORKING WITH AN ANARCHIST PUBLISHER. EASTMAN WENT FROM EDITING THE RADICAL *MASSES* MAGAZINE TO BEING A CONSERVATIVE EDITOR AT *READER'S DIGEST*.

26

HORKHEIMER IMMEDIATELY SET THE INSTITUTE ON A NEW COURSE.

WE ARE NOT OPTIMISTS OR PESSIMISTS. OUR **CRITICAL THEORY** CUTS THROUGH THE RATIONALIZATION OF WHAT IS, BUT IT CANNOT ASSUME WHAT WILL BE.

OUR CRITIQUE IS **MATERIALIST** SO IT MUST CONTINUE TO RELY ON **EMPIRICAL WORK**.

TO THAT END, I PROPOSE A EUROPE-WIDE STUDY OF WORKERS' ATTITUDES TOWARDS POLITICS.

POLICE LINE • DO NOT CROSS

ERICH FROMM & PAUL LAZARSFELD, TWO NEWER INSTITUTE MEMBERS, WERE PUT IN CHARGE OF THE STUDY.

WE GAVE OUT OVER 3000 QUESTIONNAIRES TO WORKERS & EMPLOYEES IN THE RHINELAND. THAT'S A GOOD START.

AND WE GOT BACK 586 AND— UH—

I GUESS THAT WILL HAVE TO BE IT!

TIME TO GO!

THE INSTITUTE HAD SET UP A BRANCH OFFICE IN GENEVA TO HELP WITH RESEARCH IN OTHER PARTS OF EUROPE, BUT ALSO WITH AN EYE ON THE GROWING FASCIST THREAT.

MARCH 1933:

SAVE WHAT CAN BE SAVED!

INCLUDING 586 QUESTIONNAIRES WHICH TELL US—?

THAT MANY GERMAN WORKERS WHO IDENTIFY WITH THE LEFT NEVERTHELESS HAVE AUTHORITARIAN PERSONALITIES.

I KNEW THAT.

DIE GEDANKEN SIND FREI

GERMANY SWITZERLAND

GENEVA

INSTITUTE FOR SOCIAL...

"DIE GEDANKEN SIND FREI" = THOUGHTS ARE FREE

THE LÖWENTHALS AND HORKHEIMERS WERE THE LAST TO LEAVE FRANKFURT BEFORE—

CLOSED DUE TO TENDENCIES HOSTILE TO THE STATE

NOW THE REVOLUTIONARY MERGES WITH THE REFUGEE, PREPARED TO GRASP A CRITIQUE THAT A COMFORTABLE MIND CANNOT IMAGINE.

27

CHAPTER 4

THE SWINE OF 117TH STREET

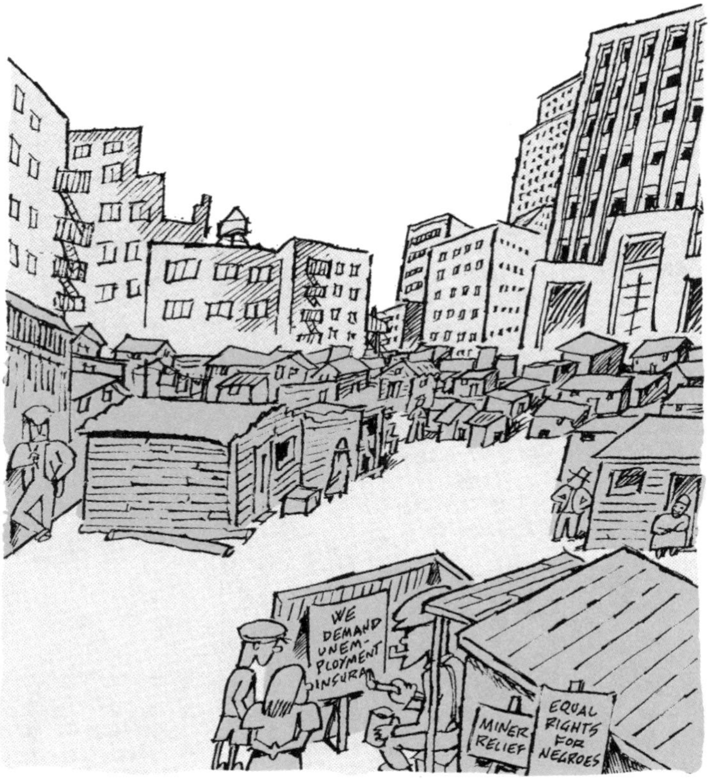
WE DEMAND UNEM-PLOYMENT INSURA
MINER RELIEF
EQUAL RIGHTS FOR NEGROES

MAY 1933

POW!!

ZIP!

MARCUSE IN GENEVA GETS THE NEWS: HEIDEGGER HAS JOINED THE NAZI PARTY & IS LEADING FREIBURG UNIVERSITY.

LET NOT DOCTRINE & "IDEAS" BE THE RULE OF YOUR BEING!

TODAY & IN THE FUTURE, ONLY THE FÜHRER HIMSELF IS GERMAN REALITY & LAW!

SEMITIC NOMADS WILL NEVER UNDERSTAND OUR GERMAN SPACE!

SO MUCH FOR "HEIDEGGEREAN MARXISM."

IT'S NOT JUST GERMANY. WE THOUGHT SWITZERLAND WOULD BE SAFE BUT LOOK AT THESE PEOPLE.

NEWSREEL TONIGHT: IRRESISTIBLE FASCISM

I'M OFF TO NEW YORK CITY TOMORROW.

MAYBE WE CAN SET UP SHOP THERE.

PRESIDENT COLUMBIA UNIVERSITY

I'M SORRY, MY ENGLISH IS NOT SO GOOD. DID YOU JUST SAY WE COULD BECOME PART OF COLUMBIA?

YOU HAVE UNDERSTOOD ME PERFECTLY.

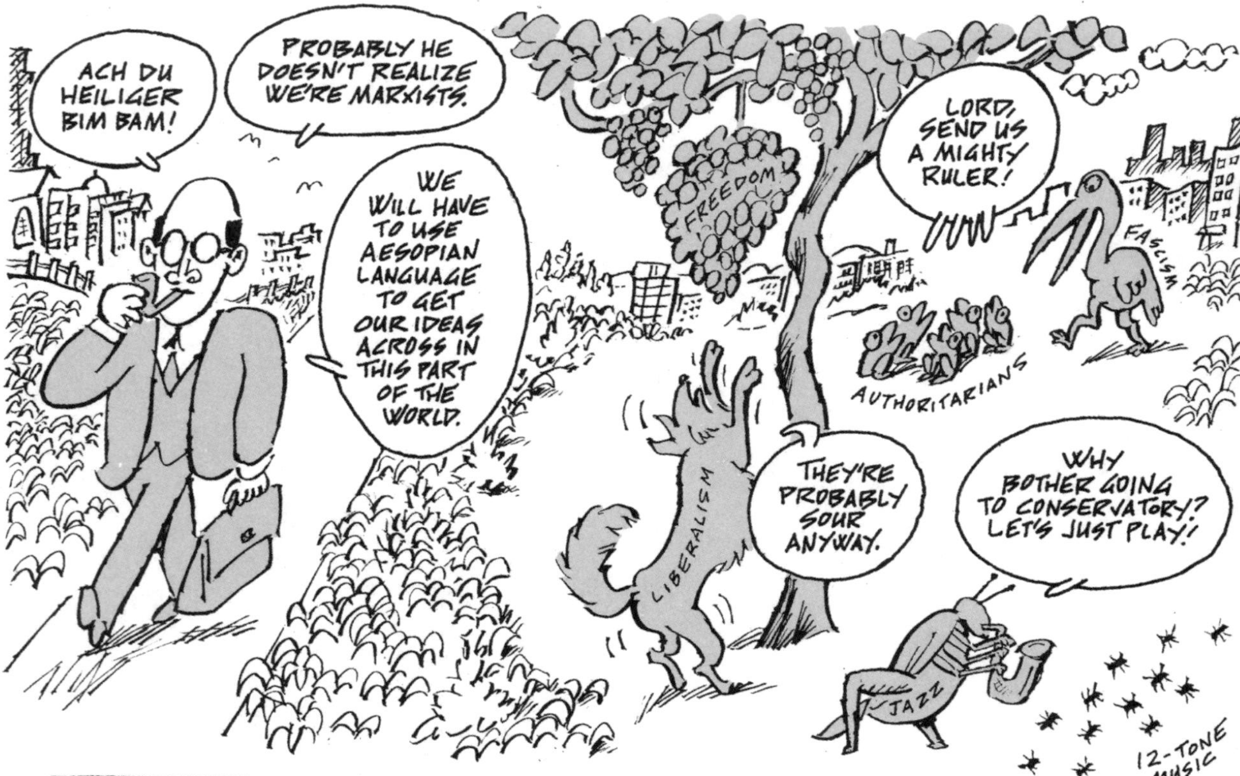
ACH DU HEILIGER BIM BAM!
PROBABLY HE DOESN'T REALIZE WE'RE MARXISTS.
WE WILL HAVE TO USE AESOPIAN LANGUAGE TO GET OUR IDEAS ACROSS IN THIS PART OF THE WORLD.
FREEDOM
LIBERALISM
THEY'RE PROBABLY SOUR ANYWAY.
LORD, SEND US A MIGHTY RULER!
AUTHORITARIANS
FASCISM
WHY BOTHER GOING TO CONSERVATORY? LET'S JUST PLAY!
JAZZ
12-TONE MUSIC

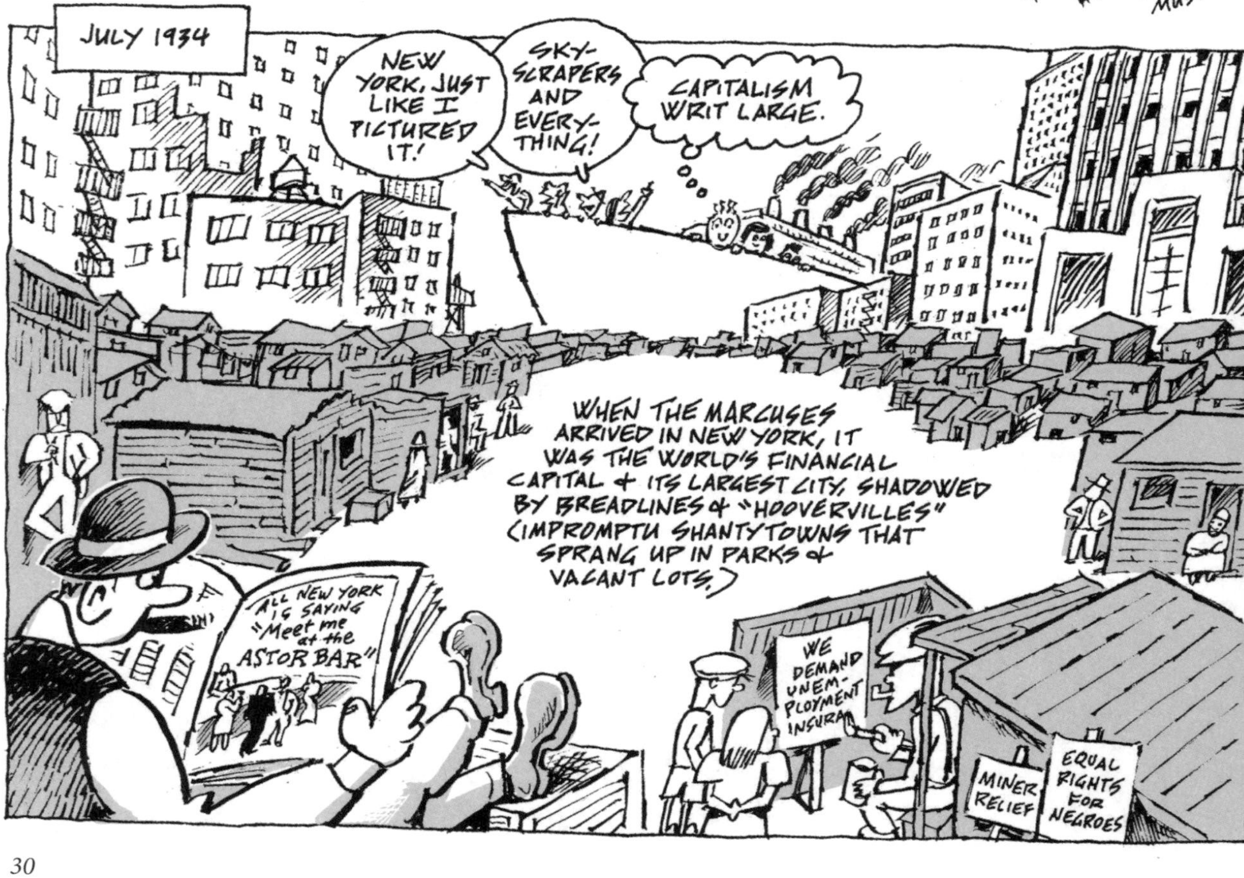
JULY 1934
NEW YORK, JUST LIKE I PICTURED IT!
SKY-SCRAPERS AND EVERY-THING!
CAPITALISM WRIT LARGE.
WHEN THE MARCUSES ARRIVED IN NEW YORK, IT WAS THE WORLD'S FINANCIAL CAPITAL & ITS LARGEST CITY, SHADOWED BY BREADLINES & "HOOVERVILLES" (IMPROMPTU SHANTYTOWNS THAT SPRANG UP IN PARKS & VACANT LOTS.)
ALL NEW YORK IS SAYING "Meet me at the ASTOR BAR"
WE DEMAND UNEM-PLOYMENT INSURA
MINER RELIEF
EQUAL RIGHTS FOR NEGROES

YES, COLUMBIA FOUND US THIS BEAUTIFUL PLACE TWO BLOCKS FROM THE CAMPUS.

I GUESS THIS IS WHEN YOU'RE SUPPOSED TO COUNT YOUR BLESSINGS.

NOW THAT THE WITTFOGELS* ARE HERE, THE ENTIRE INSTITUTE IS SAFELY OUT OF EUROPE.

I JUST WISH WE COULD GET WALTER BENJAMIN** TO COME TO NEW YORK.

PETER! DON'T BOTHER YOUR FATHER WHEN HE'S WORKING!

* KARL WITTFOGEL, A FOUNDING MEMBER OF THE INSTITUTE, WAS FREED FROM A NAZI CONCENTRATION CAMP THANKS TO AN INTERNATIONAL CAMPAIGN.

** WALTER BENJAMIN, CLOSE TO THE INSTITUTE THOUGH NEVER A MEMBER, LIVED IN PARIS AFTER FLEEING GERMANY.

MARCUSE IN NEW YORK THREW HIMSELF INTO WRITING REVIEWS & ESSAYS FOR THE ZEITSCHRIFT FÜR SOZIALFORSCHUNG, THE INSTITUTE'S JOURNAL, WITH THE OBJECT OF

IDENTIFYING THE TENDENCIES THAT LINKED THE LIBERAL PAST TO ITS TOTALITARIAN ABOLITION.

IN "THE STRUGGLE AGAINST LIBERALISM IN THE TOTALITARIAN VIEW OF THE STATE," HE SCOFFED AT THE NAZIS' ANTI-LIBERAL POLEMICS.

YOUR RATIONALISM IS NO MATCH FOR OUR GERMAN BLOOD AND GERMAN SOIL!

YOUR INDIVIDUALISM WILL NOT UNDERMINE OUR MASS MOVEMENT!

MODERN (MONOPOLY CAPITALIST) LIBERALISM

FATHER KNOWS BEST

CLASSIC LIBERALISM

BEATING A DEAD HORSE

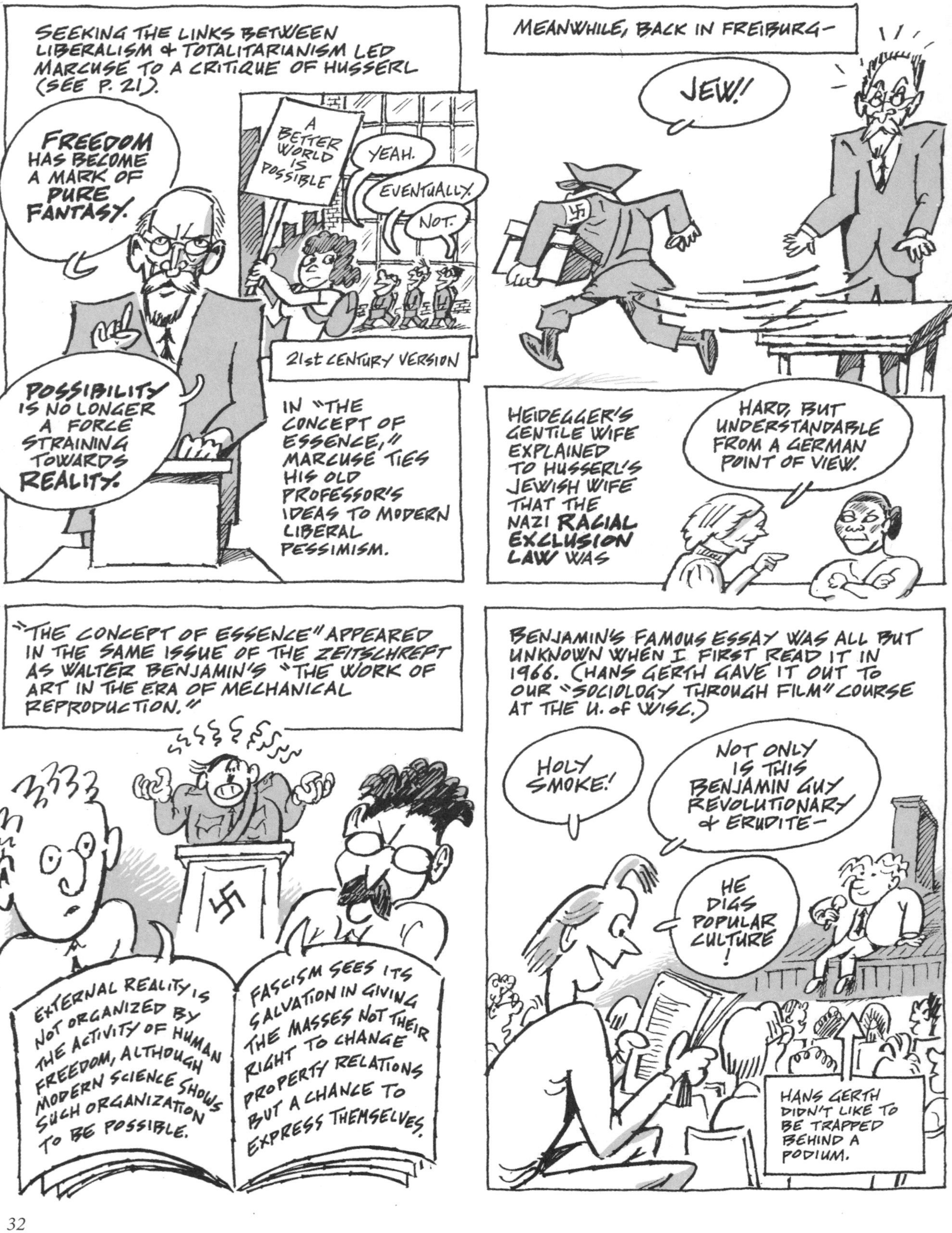
SEEKING THE LINKS BETWEEN LIBERALISM & TOTALITARIANISM LED MARCUSE TO A CRITIQUE OF HUSSERL (SEE P. 21).
FREEDOM HAS BECOME A MARK OF PURE FANTASY.
A BETTER WORLD IS POSSIBLE
YEAH.
EVENTUALLY.
NOT.
21st CENTURY VERSION
POSSIBILITY IS NO LONGER A FORCE STRAINING TOWARDS REALITY.
IN "THE CONCEPT OF ESSENCE," MARCUSE TIES HIS OLD PROFESSOR'S IDEAS TO MODERN LIBERAL PESSIMISM.
MEANWHILE, BACK IN FREIBURG-
JEW!
HEIDEGGER'S GENTILE WIFE EXPLAINED TO HUSSERL'S JEWISH WIFE THAT THE NAZI RACIAL EXCLUSION LAW WAS
HARD, BUT UNDERSTANDABLE FROM A GERMAN POINT OF VIEW.
"THE CONCEPT OF ESSENCE" APPEARED IN THE SAME ISSUE OF THE ZEITSCHREFT AS WALTER BENJAMIN'S "THE WORK OF ART IN THE ERA OF MECHANICAL REPRODUCTION."
EXTERNAL REALITY IS NOT ORGANIZED BY THE ACTIVITY OF HUMAN FREEDOM, ALTHOUGH MODERN SCIENCE SHOWS SUCH ORGANIZATION TO BE POSSIBLE.
FASCISM SEES ITS SALVATION IN GIVING THE MASSES NOT THEIR RIGHT TO CHANGE PROPERTY RELATIONS BUT A CHANCE TO EXPRESS THEMSELVES.
BENJAMIN'S FAMOUS ESSAY WAS ALL BUT UNKNOWN WHEN I FIRST READ IT IN 1966. (HANS GERTH GAVE IT OUT TO OUR "SOCIOLOGY THROUGH FILM" COURSE AT THE U. of WISC.)
HOLY SMOKE!
NOT ONLY IS THIS BENJAMIN GUY REVOLUTIONARY & ERUDITE-
HE DIGS POPULAR CULTURE!
HANS GERTH DIDN'T LIKE TO BE TRAPPED BEHIND A PODIUM.

HANNAH ARENDT CRITICIZED THE INSTITUTE IN 1965 FOR IMPOSING "SUGGESTIONS" ON BENJAMIN, BUT LEO LÖWENTHAL REMEMBERED IT DIFFERENTLY.

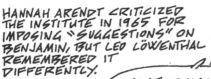

NONE OF US WAS SPARED!

MEET THE **INSTITUTE**

WE MEAN THIS IN A DIFFERENT SENSE.

IS THIS HOW WE MEAN THE DIALECTIC?

WTF?

WE DO NOT USE SUCH AN EXPRESSION.

THE COMMITMENT TO A "WE"—A COLLECTIVE VOICE—WAS DRIVEN BY THE TASK AT HAND.

WE WERE ALL POSSESSED, SO TO SPEAK, OF THE IDEA WE MUST BEAT HITLER & FASCISM, & THIS BROUGHT US TOGETHER.

THAT INCLUDED ALL THE SECRETARIES & ALL COMING TO THE INSTITUTE & WORKING THERE.

THIS MISSION GAVE US A SENSE OF LOYALTY & BELONGING.

ALICE MEYER, HORKHEIMER'S SECRETARY

ANTI-FASCIST UNITY FELT LIKE A HARBINGER OF THINGS TO COME.

LIBERATION

MOST RADICAL EMIGRÉS THOUGHT FASCISM WOULD BE DEFEATED BY A REVOLUTIONARY COALITION OF ALL DEMOCRATIC FORCES.

APOLOGIES TO DELACROIX & CALVO & DANCETTE

BUT IN LATER YEARS, MARCUSE WOULD SAY OF THE 1930s:

THE END OF A HISTORICAL PERIOD & THE HORRORS OF THE ONE TO COME WERE ANNOUNCED IN THE SIMULTANEITY OF THE CIVIL WAR IN SPAIN & THE TRIALS IN MOSCOW.

SPAIN

THE FASCISTS ARE UNITED AGAINST US. WHY WON'T THE DEMOCRACIES HELP US OUT?

TOO MUCH LIBERATION.

MOSCOW

YOUR FRIEND IS SUCH A BRILLIANT REVOLUTIONIST. LET'S LOOK HIM UP.

CAN'T.

WHY NOT?

SHOT.

THE MOSCOW TRIALS, WHEN STALIN & HIS CLIQUE BEGAN KILLING OFF THEIR FORMER COMRADES, SPLIT THE INSTITUTE.

AROUND THE TIME WITTFOGEL BROKE WITH THE INSTITUTE, ANOTHER GERMAN REFUGEE APPEARED ON THE SCENE.

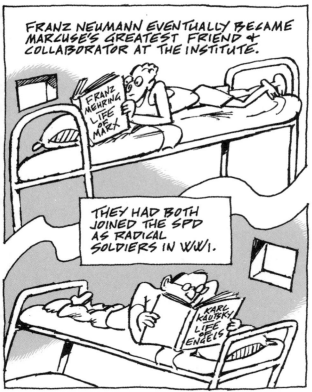

FRANZ NEUMANN EVENTUALLY BECAME MARCUSE'S GREATEST FRIEND & COLLABORATOR AT THE INSTITUTE.

FRANZ MEHRING LIFE OF MARX

THEY HAD BOTH JOINED THE SPD AS RADICAL SOLDIERS IN WWI.

KARL KAUTSKY LIFE OF ENGELS

UNLIKE MARCUSE, NEUMANN STUCK WITH THE SPD (AS A LABOR LAWYER), BUT HE CAME TO REGRET IT.

HOW **LYING** THE SPD WAS IN THE MONTHS BETWEEN JULY 1932 & MAY 1933 (& NOT ONLY THEN) I SAW WITH **MY OWN EYES** — BUT I SAID NOTHING.

HOW **COWARDLY** THE UNION BOSSES WERE — AND I CONTINUED TO SERVE THEM.

1939

THE WAR IS MAKING PEOPLE CRAZY.

AUSTRIA FALLS
CZECHOSLOVAKIA FALLS
SPAIN FALLS
POLAND FALLS

HITLER USES ANTI-RATIONAL APPEALS TO SPIRIT, SOUL, AND LEADER TO MOBILIZE MY COUNTRYMEN FOR CONQUEST—

—WHILE HORKHEIMER & ADORNO TALK ABOUT THE **TYRANNY OF REASON.**

ZEITSCHRIFT

BLITZKRIEG!

SOME WRITERS SEEM TO THINK HEGEL WAS THE INVENTOR OF FASCISM.

HE WAS THE OPPOSITE!

SHEESH!

SIDNEY HOOK

BERTRAND RUSSELL

ALDOUS HUXLEY

I NEED TO WORK OUT MY IDEAS ON HEGEL, & REASON, & REVOLUTION—

& WRITE THEM UP IN ENGLISH.

YOUR ENGLISH IS BETTER THAN MINE, SOPHIE. CAN YOU HELP ME WITH THIS?

MARCUSE'S 1941 BOOK, REASON & REVOLUTION, DISPOSES WITH THE IDEA OF HEGEL AS A PROTO-FASCIST, WHICH WAS BASED ON HEGEL'S SUPPORT FOR THE AUTHORITARIAN PRUSSIAN STATE.

PROTO-FASCIST? I DON'T THINK SO.

♪ I LOVE TO GO A-WANDERING, TO TRACK THE MOUNTAIN VIEWS AND AS I GO, I LOVE TO SMACK SUBHUMAN SLAVS & JEWS! ♪

HEGEL WAS SHARPLY CRITICAL OF THE "GERMAN YOUTH MOVEMENT"—PRECURSORS OF HITLER YOUTH—FOR ITS RACISM.

AND HIS SUPPORT FOR A STRONG STATE WAS BASED ON ITS MEDIATING ROLE BETWEEN CAPITAL & LABOR—

—NOTHING LIKE THE FASCISTS' LOVE FOR UNENCUMBERED CAPITAL.

GOTCHA

REASON & REVOLUTION TIES HEGEL INSTEAD TO SOCIALISM.

LABOR MEANS FREEDOM FROM NATURE'S CAPRICE.

BUT IT CAN ALSO MEAN THE COMPLETE SUBORDINATION OF THE INDIVIDUAL TO THE **DEMON OF ABSTRACT LABOR.**

THE MORE THE WORKER SUBJUGATES HIS LABOR TO MACHINERY, THE MORE POWERLESS HE BECOMES.

GIMME!

THE TONE & PATHOS OF THE DESCRIPTIONS POINT STRIKINGLY TO MARX'S CAPITAL.

IN FACT, REASON & REVOLUTION TRACES THE ARC THAT JOINS THE REVOLUTIONARY LIBERALISM OF 1789 TO MARXIAN SOCIALISM, WITH HEGEL AS THE KEYSTONE.

(REMEMBER, THE BOOK CAME OUT IN 1941, THE YEAR HITLER'S INVASION OF THE USSR REUNITED ANTI-FASCIST FORCES.)

ACCORDING TO HEGEL, *REASON* MAKES REVOLUTION NECESSARY.

ALL FICTIONS DISAPPEAR BEFORE TRUTH.

ROBESPIERRE

• FRENCH REVOLUTION 1789 •

OPPRESSION DROVE MEN TO **INVESTIGATION.**

NEVER BEFORE HAD IT BEEN PERCEIVED THAT MAN'S EXISTENCE CENTERS **IN HIS HEAD.**

& THAT **THOUGHT** OUGHT TO GOVERN SPIRITUAL REALITY.

THIS WAS ACCORDINGLY A **GLORIOUS MENTAL DAWN!**

37

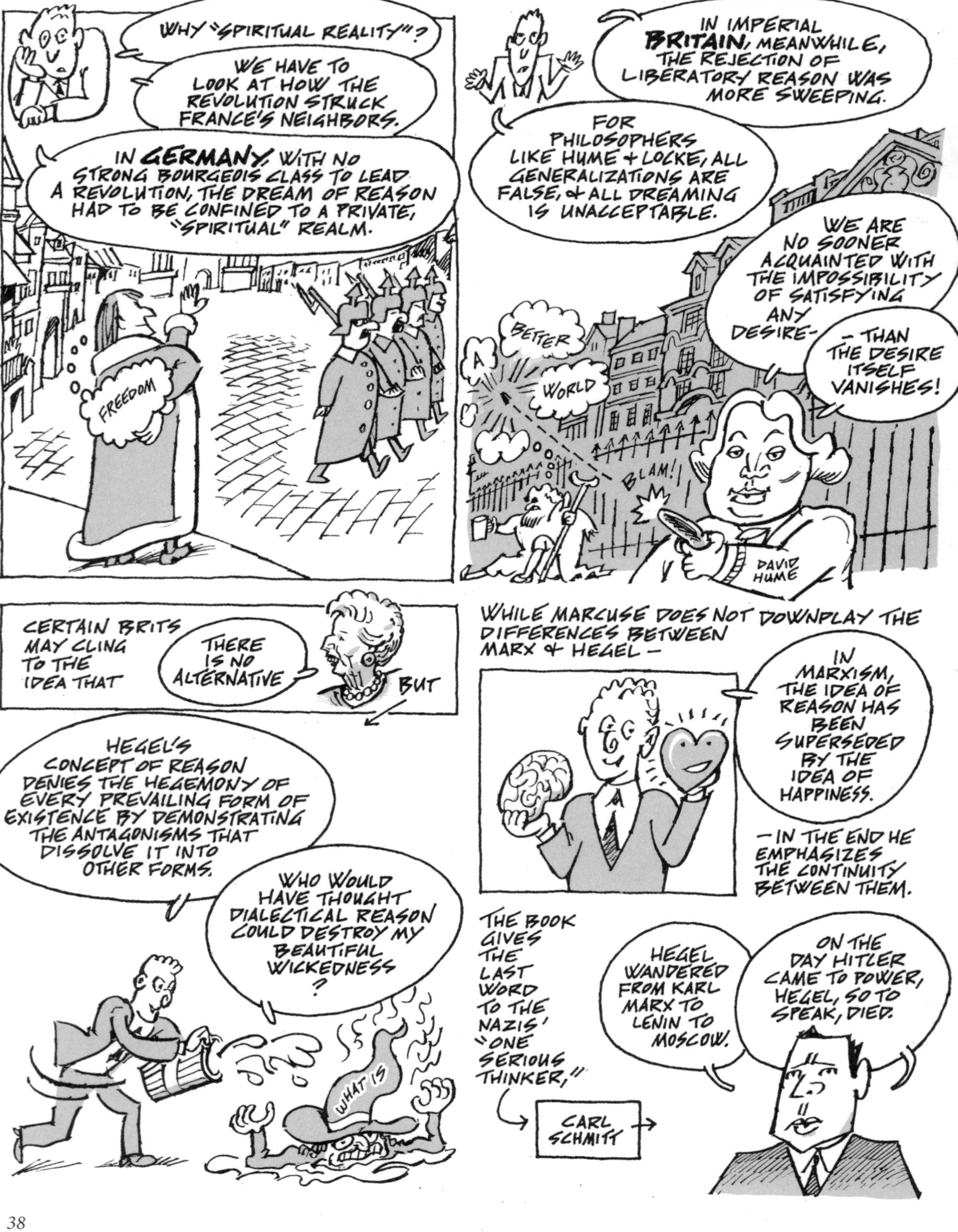
WHY "SPIRITUAL REALITY"?
WE HAVE TO LOOK AT HOW THE REVOLUTION STRUCK FRANCE'S NEIGHBORS.
IN GERMANY, WITH NO STRONG BOURGEOIS CLASS TO LEAD A REVOLUTION, THE DREAM OF REASON HAD TO BE CONFINED TO A PRIVATE, "SPIRITUAL" REALM.
FREEDOM
IN IMPERIAL BRITAIN, MEANWHILE, THE REJECTION OF LIBERATORY REASON WAS MORE SWEEPING.
FOR PHILOSOPHERS LIKE HUME + LOCKE, ALL GENERALIZATIONS ARE FALSE, + ALL DREAMING IS UNACCEPTABLE.
A BETTER WORLD
WE ARE NO SOONER ACQUAINTED WITH THE IMPOSSIBILITY OF SATISFYING ANY DESIRE-
-THAN THE DESIRE ITSELF VANISHES!
BLAM!
DAVID HUME
CERTAIN BRITS MAY CLING TO THE IDEA THAT
THERE IS NO ALTERNATIVE
BUT
HEGEL'S CONCEPT OF REASON DENIES THE HEGEMONY OF EVERY PREVAILING FORM OF EXISTENCE BY DEMONSTRATING THE ANTAGONISMS THAT DISSOLVE IT INTO OTHER FORMS.
WHO WOULD HAVE THOUGHT DIALECTICAL REASON COULD DESTROY MY BEAUTIFUL WICKEDNESS?
WHAT IS
WHILE MARCUSE DOES NOT DOWNPLAY THE DIFFERENCES BETWEEN MARX + HEGEL—
IN MARXISM, THE IDEA OF REASON HAS BEEN SUPERSEDED BY THE IDEA OF HAPPINESS.
—IN THE END HE EMPHASIZES THE CONTINUITY BETWEEN THEM.
THE BOOK GIVES THE LAST WORD TO THE NAZIS' "ONE SERIOUS THINKER,"
CARL SCHMITT
HEGEL WANDERED FROM KARL MARX TO LENIN TO MOSCOW.
ON THE DAY HITLER CAME TO POWER, HEGEL, SO TO SPEAK, DIED.

ONE OF MARCUSE'S GRAD STUDENTS TOLD ME:

REASON & REVOLUTION WAS HIS MOST IMPORTANT BOOK.

BUT WHEN I INTERVIEWED PETER MARCUSE & HIS WIFE FRANCES, I GOT A DIFFERENT ASSESSMENT.

DON'T EXAGGERATE ITS IMPORTANCE.

IT WAS DESIGNED TO ESTABLISH HIS ACADEMIC REPUTATION.

1942

CALIFORNIA DREAMIN'! HORKHEIMER MOVES TO CALIFORNIA FOR HIS HEALTH & MOST OF THE INSTITUTE FOLLOWS— INCLUDING THE FINANCIALLY STRAPPED MARCUSES WHO SKIP OUT ON THEIR LAST MONTH'S RENT.

I DON'T THINK YOU'LL FIND ANY COCONUTS UP THERE, PETER.

RIVERSIDE DRIVE, NYC

18th STREET, SANTA MONICA

THE PACIFIC OCEAN, JUST LIKE I PICTURED IT.

WE SHOULD THROW OUT A MESSAGE IN A BOTTLE.

IT SHOULD SAY, "I FEEL SO LOUSY."

THE EXILE COMMUNITY IN WEST LOS ANGELES INCLUDED THE MARCUSES' SANTA MONICA BUNGALOW AS WELL AS THE HORKHEIMERS' FABULOUS HOME IN PACIFIC PALISADES.

KURT WEILL

LOTTE LENYA

GERTRUD SCHOENBERG

THOMAS MANN

ARNOLD SCHOENBERG

HELENE WEGEL

MARLENE DIETRICH

ERICH MARIE REMARQUE

FRITZ LANG

ALFRED DÜBLIN

MAX REINHART

AH, MARCUSE, YOU CAME.

REMEMBER, BEST BEHAVIOR.

LOOKS LIKE WALLACE SHAWN & ANDRE GREGORY BUT IT'S HANNS EISLER & BERTOLT BRECHT

YES, THAT'S THE SAME FRITZ LANG WE MET IN CHAPTER 2.

LANG'S LAST DAY IN GERMANY WAS IN 1941. HE WAS SUMMONED TO THE OFFICE OF JOSEF GOEBBELS.

THE FATHERLAND NEEDS GREAT CINEMA, MR. LANG. YOU ARE TO BE MADE HEAD OF UFA, GERMANY'S LARGEST FILM STUDIO!

TO YOU I WILL GIVE ALL AUTHORITY & GLORY!!

FOR IT HAS BEEN DELIVERED TO ME, & I GIVE IT TO WHOM I WILL.

LANG FLED THE COUNTRY THAT NIGHT.

LANG IN HOLLYWOOD WORKED HIS JAUNDICED REFUGEE WORLDVIEW INTO CLASSICS OF FILM NOIR.

WELL, REFUGEES MAKE THE BEST DIALECTICAL THINKERS.

HEY, FRITZ, WHAT WOULD YOU THINK OF TRYING TO MAKE AN ANTI-NAZI FILM?

HM! NOW THAT GERMANY'S DECLARED WAR ON THE UNITED STATES, I BET WE COULD ACTUALLY BRING IT OFF!

THE BRECHT-LANG COLLABORATION, "HANGMEN ALSO DIE," WAS A DISAPPOINTMENT TO BRECHT, BUT HE MADE ENOUGH MONEY ON IT TO WRITE THREE PLAYS.

HERE'S SOMETHING ELSE BRECHT WROTE IN LOS ANGELES:

I'm told that you raised your hand against yourself
Anticipating the butcher.
After eight years in exile, observing the rise of the enemy
Then at last, brought up against the impassable frontier
You passed, they say, a passable one.

Empires collapse. Gangleaders
Are strutting about like statesmen. The peoples
Can no longer be seen under all those armaments.

So the future lies in darkness, and the forces of right
Are weak. All this was plain to you
When you destroyed a torturable body.

WALTER BENJAMIN, TRAPPED AT THE FRENCH-SPANISH BORDER, HAD KILLED HIMSELF RATHER THAN FALL INTO NAZI HANDS.

CALIFORNIA SEVERED THE CORD THAT TIED MARCUSE TO THE INSTITUTE.

REALLY, MARCUSE IS ONLY HINDERED BY JUDAISM FROM BEING A FASCIST.

WE HAVE TO CUT YOUR SALARY FROM $350 PER MONTH TO $280.

OUR ENDOWMENT IS DRYING UP. YOU MIGHT THINK ABOUT LOOKING FOR WORK ELSEWHERE.

ADORNO HORK

THE INSTITUTE

YOU HAVE A SOLID OFFER OF GOVERNMENT WORK? HELPING INTERPRET NAZIISM TO AMERICAN POLICY MAKERS? TAKE IT!

D.C. IS DREARY BUT YOU'D ACTUALLY BE FIGHTING FASCISM.

I KNOW OF NO PLACE BUT THE INSTITUTE WHERE ONE IS REALLY ENCOURAGED TO THINK.

BUT LIEBSCHEN—THEY DON'T APPRECIATE YOU!

WE'RE GOING. ALL HANDS ON DECK!

INGE NEUMANN

ADORNO & HORKHEIMER WENT ON TO COLLABORATE ON THEIR ALLEGED MASTERPIECE, *DIALECTIC OF ENLIGHTENMENT*—

"THE FULLY ENLIGHTENED EARTH RADIATES DISASTER TRIUMPHANT."

SO IT SEEMS BUT WE COULD DO BETTER.

WE DOUBT IT.

NEVER KNOW UNTIL YOU TRY.

—A BOOK MARCUSE HAD HOPED TO HAVE A HAND IN.

INSTEAD, MARCUSE & HIS INSTITUTE FRIENDS FRANZ NEUMANN & OTTO KIRCHEIMER JOINED OTHER INTELLECTUALS DOING WAR WORK AT THE OFFICE OF STRATEGIC SERVICES (OSS).

WILLIAM DONOVAN

H. STUART HUGHES

BARRINGTON MOORE

NORMAN O. BROWN

JOHN KENNETH GALBRAITH

"WILD BILL" DONOVAN, WHO ASSEMBLED THE OSS STAFF, WAS A WALL STREET REPUBLICAN, BUT HE HAD AN EYE FOR TALENT.

"IT WAS AS THOUGH THE LEFT-HEGELIAN WORLD SPIRIT HAD BRIEFLY DESCENDED ON THE CENTRAL EUROPEAN DEPARTMENT OF THE OSS."

JOHN HERTZ, ANOTHER REFUGEE SCHOLAR IN GOVERNMENT

THE FRANKFURTERS' POLICY ADVICE WAS PRACTICAL & PRESCIENT.

DON'T IMAGINE A NEGOTIATED SURRENDER LIKE IN 1918.

THE NAZIS HAVE MADE ALL OF GERMANY COMPLICIT IN THEIR CRIMES. THE GERMANS WILL FIGHT TO THE DEATH.

THEIR RECOMMENDATIONS FOR POST-WAR RECONSTRUCTION WENT UNHEEDED, HOWEVER.

ANOTHER MARCUSE GRAD STUDENT RECALLS

From: Andrew Feenberg
To: Nick Thorkelson
Re: Marcuse comic

Marcuse once told us, when he introduced Barrington Moore for a talk,

WE ATTEMPTED TO DENAZIFY GERMANY AFTER THE WAR.

WE FAILED MISERABLY.

DAILY TE_

MERKEL TO GREECE: SUBMIT OR DIE

1945: BRAVE-ISH NEW WORLD

FAR FROM BRINGING DENAZIFICATION, THE END OF THE WAR IN EUROPE REVEALED THE FULL EXTENT OF THE NAZIS' SUCCESS:

MURDER OF EUROPE'S JEWS

ARBEITER MACH FREI!

RACIALIZATION OF IDENTITY

I'M NOT RELIGIOUS. THEREFORE I'M NOT JEWISH.

I DON'T THINK IT WORKS THAT WAY ANYMORE.

LIQUIDATION OF THE SOCIALIST ALTERNATIVE

SOCIALISTS FOR SMOOTHER ROADS

SOCIALISTS FOR BETTER HOMES & GARDENS

NORMALIZATION OF NATIONALIST AGGRESSION

EVERYBODY NEEDS A COUNTRY OF THEIR OWN.

I THINK I'LL TAKE MINE FROM THE ARABS.

DESTRUCTION OF MEMORY

WELCOME TO POST-WAR GERMANY.

YOU MEAN POST-HITLER?

HITLER WHO?

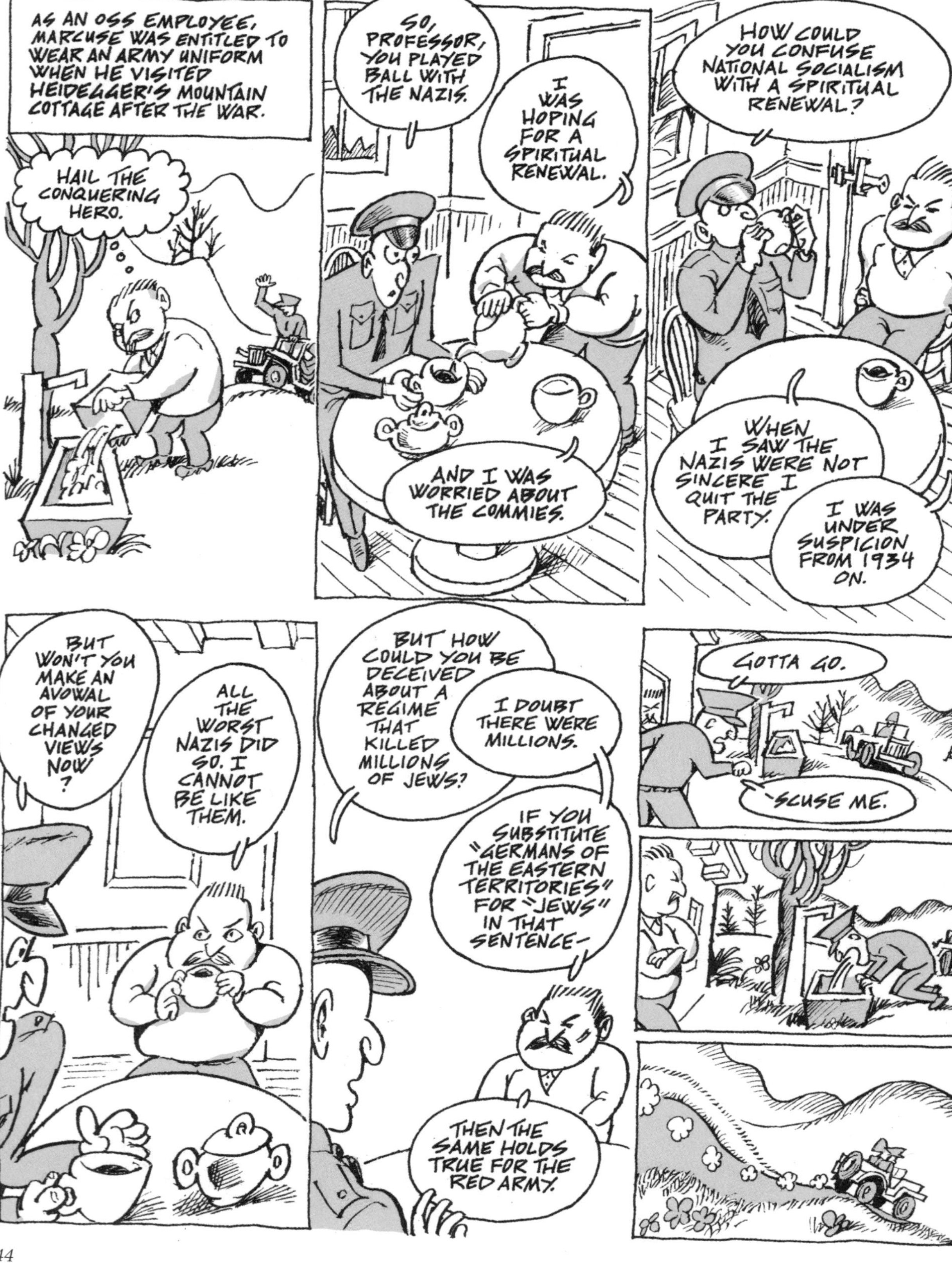

AS AN OSS EMPLOYEE, MARCUSE WAS ENTITLED TO WEAR AN ARMY UNIFORM WHEN HE VISITED HEIDEGGER'S MOUNTAIN COTTAGE AFTER THE WAR.
HAIL THE CONQUERING HERO.
SO, PROFESSOR, YOU PLAYED BALL WITH THE NAZIS.
I WAS HOPING FOR A SPIRITUAL RENEWAL.
AND I WAS WORRIED ABOUT THE COMMIES.
HOW COULD YOU CONFUSE NATIONAL SOCIALISM WITH A SPIRITUAL RENEWAL?
WHEN I SAW THE NAZIS WERE NOT SINCERE I QUIT THE PARTY.
I WAS UNDER SUSPICION FROM 1934 ON.
BUT WON'T YOU MAKE AN AVOWAL OF YOUR CHANGED VIEWS NOW?
ALL THE WORST NAZIS DID SO. I CANNOT BE LIKE THEM.
BUT HOW COULD YOU BE DECEIVED ABOUT A REGIME THAT KILLED MILLIONS OF JEWS?
I DOUBT THERE WERE MILLIONS.
IF YOU SUBSTITUTE "GERMANS OF THE EASTERN TERRITORIES" FOR "JEWS" IN THAT SENTENCE-
THEN THE SAME HOLDS TRUE FOR THE RED ARMY.
GOTTA GO.
'SCUSE ME.

BACK IN THE USA—

AS THE "GOOD WAR" GAVE WAY TO THE COLD WAR, THE OSS BECAME THE CIA, GUARANTOR OF EMPIRE!

WHAT DID THE DOCTOR SAY? GOOD NEWS I HOPE.

NOT GOOD.

THIS WOULD HAVE BEEN THE RIGHT TIME FOR MARCUSE TO LEAVE GOVERNMENT BUT SOPHIE WAS SICK & HE COULDN'T AFFORD TO.

MARCUSE WENT FROM OSS TO THE STATE DEPARTMENT, A PATRICIAN INSTITUTION THAT IGNORED HIS IDEAS.

The Soviet Union is a third-rate welfare state that will collapse of its own accord.

NO! NO! NO!

STICK TO THE SCRIPT, MARCUSE!

HE WROTE MORE BLUNTLY IN A BOOK PROPOSAL TO THE INSTITUTE, BUT NOTHING CAME OF THAT EITHER.

The world is dividing into a neo-fascist camp & a Soviet camp, though both are anti-revolutionary. But voices against the communist parties are voices against the revolution.

WACKY GUY!

STILL TALKING ABOUT THE REVOLUTION.

BY THIS TIME THE INSTITUTE HAD RETURNED TO FRANKFURT.

SOPHIE DIED IN 1951.

WE FOUND OUT SHE WAS DYING RIGHT AFTER OUR WEDDING.

LATE STAGE OVARIAN CANCER.

A HANDSOME WOMAN. SHE RAISED ME MORE THAN MY FATHER.

I LIKED HER.

SHE DIDN'T WANT TO HOVER.

MARCUSE'S MASTERY OF THE FIELD OF SOVIET STUDIES GOT HIM WORK AT THE RUSSIAN INSTITUTE AT COLUMBIA.

HE LIVED IN A SPARE ROOM AT THE NEUMANNS' HOME IN THE RIVERDALE SECTION OF THE BRONX.

FROM THERE MARCUSE MOVED TO CAMBRIDGE, MA, TO CONTINUE HIS RUSSIA RESEARCH AT HARVARD. HE RENTED A ROOM FROM SUSAN SONTAG & HER HUSBAND.

WE'RE DISCUSSING FREUD. CARE TO JOIN US?

DO I DARE TELL THEM I JUST SAW "ROCK AROUND THE CLOCK"?

AND THAT KIDS WERE DANCING IN THE AISLES?

AND I LOVED IT?

BETTER NOT.

FREUD WAS ON EVERYONE'S MIND. COLD WAR INTELLECTUALS HAD TURNED THEIR ATTENTION FROM CHANGING SOCIETY TO TAMING THE PSYCHE.

BUT—

WHAT ABOUT A BETTER WORLD?

MARCUSE HAD A DIFFERENT IDEA. HE WAS READY TO SPREAD HIS WINGS.

CHAPTER 5

EROS AND BRANDEIS

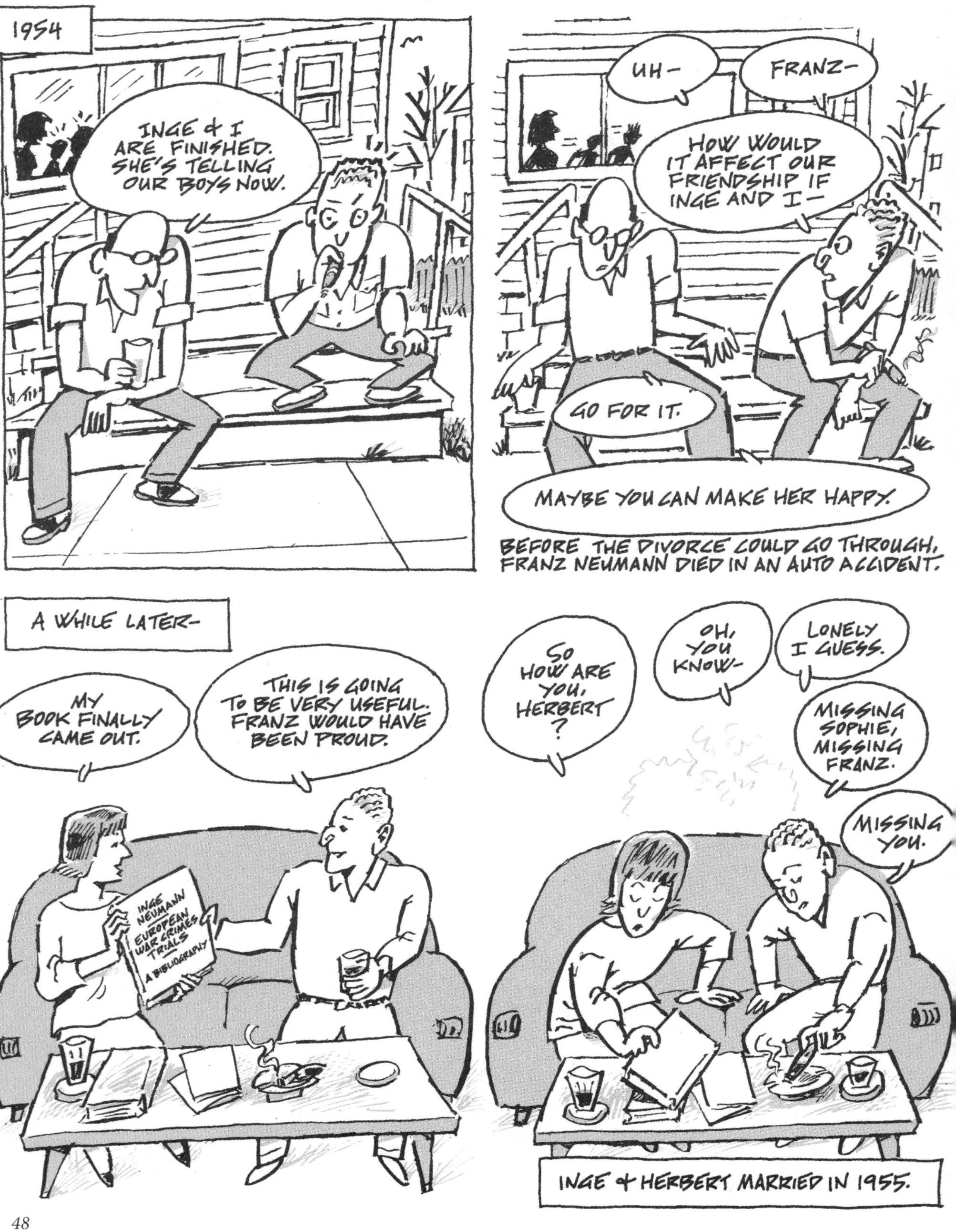
1954
INGE & I ARE FINISHED. SHE'S TELLING OUR BOYS NOW.
UH-
FRANZ-
HOW WOULD IT AFFECT OUR FRIENDSHIP IF INGE AND I—
GO FOR IT.
MAYBE YOU CAN MAKE HER HAPPY.
BEFORE THE DIVORCE COULD GO THROUGH, FRANZ NEUMANN DIED IN AN AUTO ACCIDENT.
A WHILE LATER-
MY BOOK FINALLY CAME OUT.
THIS IS GOING TO BE VERY USEFUL. FRANZ WOULD HAVE BEEN PROUD.
INGE NEUMANN
EUROPEAN WAR CRIMES TRIALS
A BIBLIOGRAPHY
SO HOW ARE YOU, HERBERT?
OH, YOU KNOW-
LONELY I GUESS.
MISSING SOPHIE, MISSING FRANZ.
MISSING YOU.
INGE & HERBERT MARRIED IN 1955.

ALSO IN 1955:

HMPH! LEADING INTELLECTUALS HEREABOUTS DO NOT ALLOW THEMSELVES TO CONTEMPLATE A LIBERATED EXISTENCE.

WHEN THEY DARE TO CRITICIZE SOCIETY, THEY BLAME ALL OF ITS SHORTCOMINGS ON THEIR MOTHERS!

FREUD HAD IT RIGHT WHEN HE PUT IT ON THE "PRIMAL FATHER"!

TROUBLE IS, FREUD COULDN'T SEE A WAY OUT!

MAYBE MY NEW BOOK WILL HELP.

ACCORDING TO EROS + CIVILIZATION

FREUD TIED THE WOES OF THE MODERN PSYCHE TO SCARCITY—

—THE IDEA THAT WE NEED HIGHLY REPRESSIVE CIVILIZATION TO KEEP US PRODUCTIVE, TO AVOID THE WAR OF EACH AGAINST ALL.

SO WE ARE TIED IN KNOTS BY THE NEED TO SUBMIT TO AUTHORITY—

BY THE NUCLEAR FAMILY—

THE THWARTING OF AGGRESSIVE & SEXUAL INSTINCTS—

ALL THE SACRIFICES THAT MAKE IT POSSIBLE FOR US TO PERFORM ALIENATED LABOR & LIVE CHEEK BY JOWL!

49

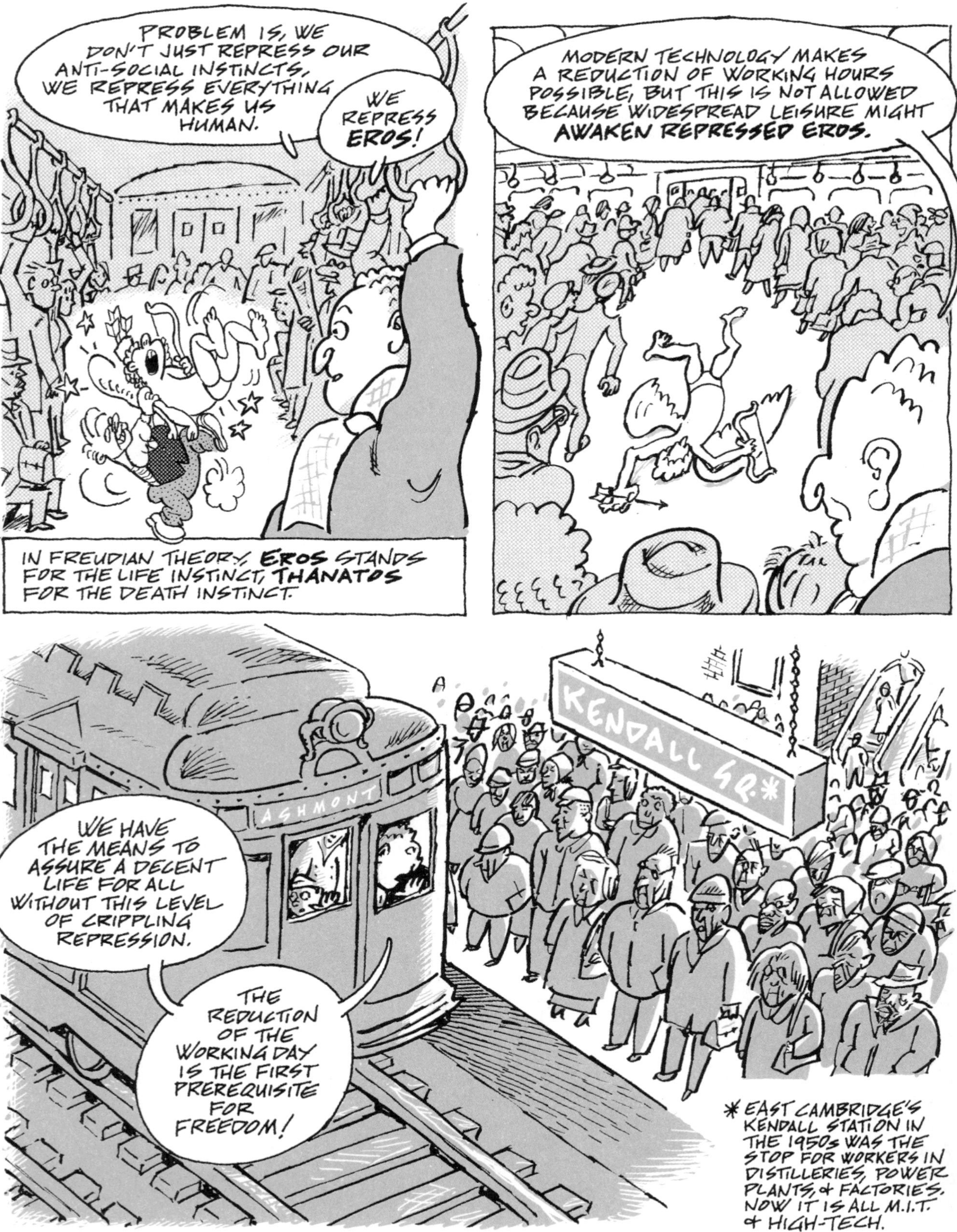
PROBLEM IS, WE DON'T JUST REPRESS OUR ANTI-SOCIAL INSTINCTS. WE REPRESS EVERYTHING THAT MAKES US HUMAN.
WE REPRESS EROS!
IN FREUDIAN THEORY, EROS STANDS FOR THE LIFE INSTINCT, THANATOS FOR THE DEATH INSTINCT.
MODERN TECHNOLOGY MAKES A REDUCTION OF WORKING HOURS POSSIBLE, BUT THIS IS NOT ALLOWED BECAUSE WIDESPREAD LEISURE MIGHT AWAKEN REPRESSED EROS.
KENDALL SQ.*
ASHMONT
WE HAVE THE MEANS TO ASSURE A DECENT LIFE FOR ALL WITHOUT THIS LEVEL OF CRIPPLING REPRESSION.
THE REDUCTION OF THE WORKING DAY IS THE FIRST PREREQUISITE FOR FREEDOM!
* EAST CAMBRIDGE'S KENDALL STATION IN THE 1950s WAS THE STOP FOR WORKERS IN DISTILLERIES, POWER PLANTS, & FACTORIES. NOW IT IS ALL M.I.T. & HIGH-TECH.

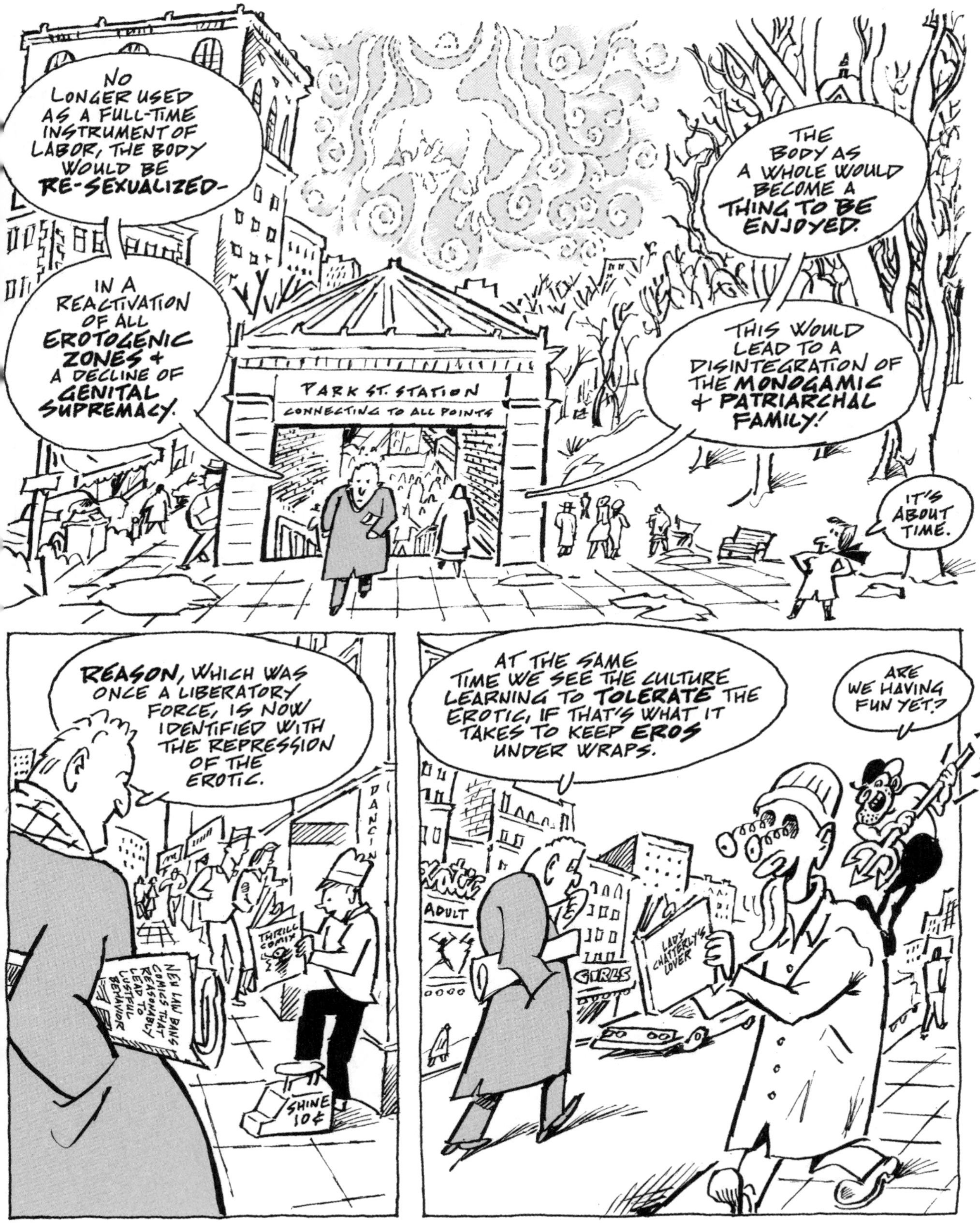

NO LONGER USED AS A FULL-TIME INSTRUMENT OF LABOR, THE BODY WOULD BE RE-SEXUALIZED-
IN A REACTIVATION OF ALL EROTOGENIC ZONES & A DECLINE OF GENITAL SUPREMACY.
PARK ST. STATION
CONNECTING TO ALL POINTS
THE BODY AS A WHOLE WOULD BECOME A THING TO BE ENJOYED.
THIS WOULD LEAD TO A DISINTEGRATION OF THE MONOGAMIC & PATRIARCHAL FAMILY!
IT'S ABOUT TIME.
REASON, WHICH WAS ONCE A LIBERATORY FORCE, IS NOW IDENTIFIED WITH THE REPRESSION OF THE EROTIC.
DANCIN
NEW LAW BANS COMICS THAT REASONABLY LEAD TO LUSTFUL BEHAVIOR
THRILL COMIX
SHINE 10¢
AT THE SAME TIME WE SEE THE CULTURE LEARNING TO TOLERATE THE EROTIC, IF THAT'S WHAT IT TAKES TO KEEP EROS UNDER WRAPS.
ARE WE HAVING FUN YET?
ADULT
GIRLS
LADY CHATTERLY'S LOVER

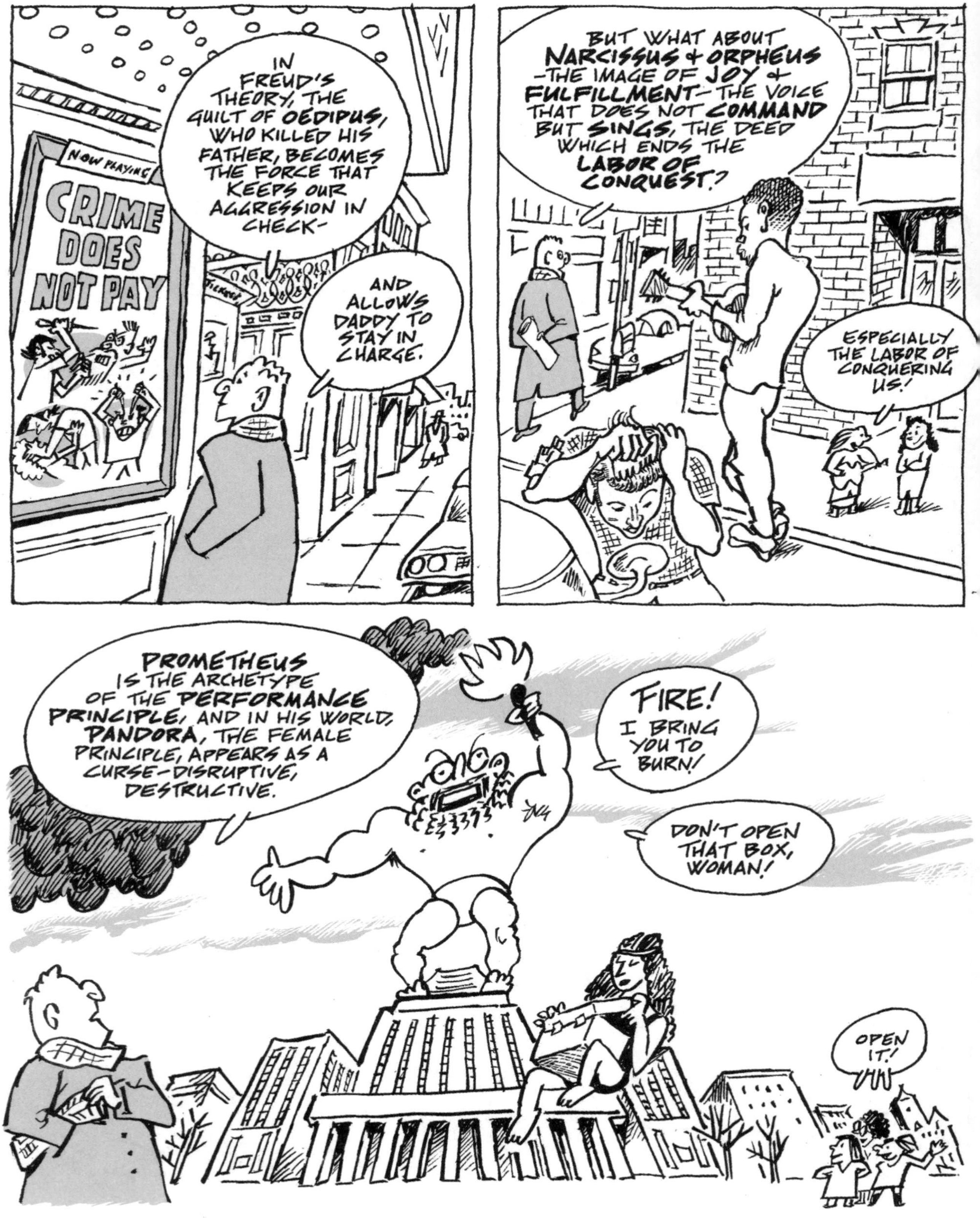
NOW PLAYING
CRIME DOES NOT PAY
IN FREUD'S THEORY, THE GUILT OF OEDIPUS, WHO KILLED HIS FATHER, BECOMES THE FORCE THAT KEEPS OUR AGGRESSION IN CHECK-
AND ALLOWS DADDY TO STAY IN CHARGE.
BUT WHAT ABOUT NARCISSUS & ORPHEUS -THE IMAGE OF JOY & FULFILLMENT- THE VOICE THAT DOES NOT COMMAND BUT SINGS, THE DEED WHICH ENDS THE LABOR OF CONQUEST?
ESPECIALLY THE LABOR OF CONQUERING US!
PROMETHEUS IS THE ARCHETYPE OF THE PERFORMANCE PRINCIPLE, AND IN HIS WORLD, PANDORA, THE FEMALE PRINCIPLE, APPEARS AS A CURSE-DISRUPTIVE, DESTRUCTIVE.
FIRE! I BRING YOU TO BURN!
DON'T OPEN THAT BOX, WOMAN!
OPEN IT!

FOR FURTHER ADVENTURES OF "THE AESTHETIC DIMENSION," SEE CHAPTER 7.

THE EPILOGUE TO *EROS & CIVILIZATION* CRITICIZED MARCUSE'S OLD INSTITUTE COLLEAGUE, ERICH FROMM, & THIS LED TO AN EXCHANGE OF POLEMICS.

(FROMM HAD BEEN DISMISSED FROM THE INSTITUTE IN 1932 FOR "MELIORISM"—ADVOCATING ADJUSTMENT RATHER THAN REBELLION—BUT HE & MARCUSE HAD REMAINED FRIENDS.)

YOU WON'T FIND A "RADICALISM INSTINCT" IN FREUD, OLD PAL, I CAN ASSURE YOU OF THAT.

NEVER SAID YOU COULD. BUT FREUD KNEW THE SUPPRESSION OF INSTINCT IS BAD FOR US.

YOU THINK FREUD SAW **LOVE** AS MERE SEXUAL DESIRE! THAT'S SICK!

FREUD'S IDEA WAS THAT LOVE **MODIFIES** DESIRE BY COMBINING IT WITH TENDERNESS & AFFECTION. HOW IS THAT A BAD THING?

YOU THINK WORKERS NEED TO SEIZE FACTORIES. BUT LOOK AT THE NEW WORKER-MANAGEMENT COUNCILS IN FRANCE. THAT'S HOW YOU DIMINISH ALIENATION!

THE FRENCH COOPS ACCEPT THE BIBLICAL INJUNCTION TO SUFFER FOR YOUR SUPPER. NOT MY IDEA OF LIBERATION!

YOU NEGLECT HUMAN HAPPINESS!

I BELIEVE **YOU** DO THAT, BY ADVOCATING "POSITIVE THINKING," & LEAVING REPRESSIVE FORCES IN CONTROL!

YOU'RE A NIHILIST! YOU JUST WANT TO TEAR THINGS DOWN!

SORT OF, YEAH!

THE DEBATE ENDED THEIR FRIENDSHIP.

WHILE MARCUSE'S IDEAS WERE CHALLENGING TO HIS PEERS, HIS **STUBBORN UTOPIANISM** EXCITED A YOUNGER GENERATION OF REBEL WOMEN.

AMERICAN FREUDIANS ARE FIXATED ON **OEDIPUS**—THE EXEMPLAR OF **GUILT** AND **PATRIARCHY**.

BUT **THIS GUY** WANTS TO TALK ABOUT THE **PRE-OEDIPAL** NURTURING **MOTHER** RATHER THAN THE PHALLUS-WIELDING **POWERFUL FATHER.**

AND LISTEN TO THIS: "THE ORGANIZATION OF SEXUALITY MIRRORS THE ORGANIZATION OF SOCIETY, SO A **STRIKE AGAINST ONE** NECESSARILY **UNDERMINES THE OTHER!**

EROS and CIVILIZATION

EROS and CIVILIZATION

HERBERT MARCUSE

THE PERSONAL IS POLITICAL, YOU MIGHT SAY.

MARCUSE RETURNED THE COMPLIMENT WHEN HE ADDED A "POLITICAL PREFACE" TO THE BOOK'S SECOND EDITION IN 1966.

BY NATURE, THE **YOUNG** ARE IN THE FOREFRONT OF THOSE WHO FIGHT AGAINST A CIVILIZATION THAT STRIVES TO SHORTEN THE "DETOUR TO DEATH."

THE FIGHT FOR EROS IS A POLITICAL FIGHT!

NO HUMAN BEING IS ILLEGAL

DISARM HATE

BLACK LIVES MATTER

PROTECT WATER

PUSSY GRABS BACK!

EROS & CIVILIZATION APPEARED JUST AS MARCUSE BEGAN HIS ACADEMIC CAREER, AT A UNIVERSITY 50 YEARS YOUNGER THAN HIMSELF.

YOU'RE APPLYING TO BRANDEIS? ISN'T THAT PLACE JEWISH?

IT'S A NON-SECTARIAN UNIVERSITY, DAD, ESTABLISHED TO MAKE UP FOR THE OPENLY ANTI-SEMITIC ADMISSIONS POLICIES OF MOST U.S. COLLEGES.

PLUTOCRAT

RESTLESS YOUTH

OK, SURE, "NON-SECTARIAN." HA HA. WHY WOULD YOU ATTEND A JEWISH COLLEGE?

HERBERT MARCUSE.

ALBERT EINSTEIN WAS THE FIGUREHEAD WHOSE NAME EXPEDITED FUNDRAISING DURING BRANDEIS'S PLANNING STAGES. HE RESIGNED FROM THE BOARD IN 1948 WHEN THEY REJECTED HIS CHOICE TO BE FIRST PRESIDENT, HAROLD LASKI,* IN FAVOR OF A FAIRLY CONSERVATIVE ZIONIST, ABRAM SACHAR.

* LASKI WAS FRANZ NEUMANN'S MENTOR IN LONDON. SEE P. 34.

ABRAM L. SACHAR WAS THE TOUGH GUY WHO BUILT UP BRANDEIS FROM NOTHING, & RECRUITED OUTLIERS LIKE MARCUSE (A KNOWN MARXIST) & ELEANOR ROOSEVELT (NOT A COLLEGE GRADUATE) TO TEACH THERE.

IN 1958, MARCUSE'S REFLECTIONS ON HIS RUSSIA RESEARCH APPEARED IN BOOK FORM. *SOVIET MARXISM* MANAGED TO PISS OFF COLD WAR PARTISANS EAST & WEST.

IN PROFESSOR MARCUSE'S MYTHOLOGY, THE SOVIET UNION IS A STAGE IN MANKIND'S STRUGGLE FOR FREEDOM & SOCIALISM.

IDIOT!

ACCORDING TO MARCUSE'S LUNATIC UTOPIANISM, SOVIET SOCIETY & CAPITALISM AMOUNT TO THE SAME THING.

JERK!

THE BOOK FAULTS THE SOVIET SYSTEM FOR ALLOWING **DEVELOPMENT** TO PUSH ASIDE SOCIALISM'S LIBERATORY PROMISE.

PROGRESS IN INDUSTRIALIZATION IS TANTAMOUNT TO PROGRESS IN DOMINATION.

AUTONOMY & SPONTANEITY ARE CONFINED TO THE LEVEL OF EFFICIENCY AND PERFORMANCE.

HARMONY BETWEEN THE HUMAN & THE SOCIAL NEED REMAINS A MERE PROMISE!

1,000,000 TRACTORS IN SEVEN YEARS! YES!

HE TRACES THIS REPRESSIVE DEVELOPMENTALISM TO 1923, THE YEAR IT BECAME CLEAR THAT THE REVOLUTION IN CENTRAL & WESTERN EUROPE WAS FINISHED. THE SOVIETS WERE ON THEIR OWN.

WORKER CONTROL, SCHMORKER CONTROL.

WE NEED TRACTORS!

AND WE NEED SOCIAL-DEMOCRATIC GOVERNMENTS IN THE WEST THAT WILL STOP TRYING TO BEAT US UP WHILE WE DEVELOP.

SOVIET MARXISM ANTICIPATES, WITH GUARDED OPTIMISM, THE LIBERALIZING CAMPAIGNS OF DUBČEK & GORBACHEV—

RISING STANDARDS OF LIVING & A PRACTICALLY FREE DISTRIBUTION OF GOODS WILL OVERCOME THE REPRESSION IMPOSED AT EARLIER STAGES—

—BUT AS LONG AS THE EAST-WEST CONFLICT REMAINS, IT SERVES TO JUSTIFY MOBILIZATION ON A TOTALITARIAN SCALE.

THE HISTORY OF SOVIET SOCIETY SEEMS TO BE FATEFULLY LINKED TO THAT OF ITS ANTAGONIST.

—WHILE ALSO FORESEEING REAGAN'S USE OF AGGRESSIVE ARMS SPENDING TO BANKRUPT THE USSR.

THREE OF MARCUSE'S STAR STUDENTS AT BRANDEIS:

RICKY (ERICA) SHEROVER

BILL LEISS

ANGELA DAVIS

BILL LEISS FIRST ENCOUNTERED MARCUSE WHILE MEETING WITH EDGAR JOHNSON, A FACULTY ADVISOR AT BRANDEIS.

I URGE YOU TO TAKE MY SEMINAR ON "FATHERS OF THE CHURCH."

EDGAR! WHEN ARE YOU GOING TO GIVE A COURSE ON **MOTHERS** OF THE CHURCH?

RICKY SHEROVER, AS AN AMERICAN CHILD GROWING UP IN MEXICO, WAS PRIMED FOR THE "REFUGEE DIALECTIC" BY HER GERMAN COMMUNIST TUTOR.

(WHEN THE FAMILY RETURNED TO AMERICA, THE U.S. GOVERNMENT WOULD NOT ALLOW THE TUTOR TO COME WITH THEM.)

ANGELA DAVIS GREW UP IN BIRMINGHAM, ALABAMA, EPICENTER OF THE RACIST TERROR THAT THE SOUTHERN BLACK MOVEMENT HAD TO OVERCOME.

HER NEIGHBORHOOD WAS KNOWN AS "DYNAMITE HILL."

WHEN ANGELA WAS FIVE, A HOUSE ACROSS FROM HER WAS BLOWN UP WHEN A BLACK FAMILY TRIED TO MOVE IN.

* THE SCOTTSBORO DEFENDANTS WERE NINE BLACK TEENAGERS FRAMED & SENTENCED TO DIE IN 1931, WHOSE LIVES WERE SAVED BY A CAMPAIGN LED BY THE NAACP & THE COMMUNIST PARTY.

WITH HELP FROM THE ACLU, DAVIS WAS SENT TO ELIZABETH IRWIN HIGH SCHOOL IN MANHATTAN, WHERE HER JEWISH CLASSMATES ENCOURAGED HER TO ATTEND BRANDEIS.

SADA GORDON, MARCUSE'S LEGENDARY SECRETARY

FOR DAVIS, MARCUSE PROVED "IT WAS POSSIBLE TO BE AN ACADEMIC & AN ACTIVIST, A SCHOLAR + A REVOLUTIONARY."

BUT MARCUSE'S ACTIVISM TURNED BRANDEIS'S LEADERS & DONORS AGAINST HIM.

AS IF MARCUSE'S POLITICAL ACTIVITIES WERE NOT PROVOCATIVE ENOUGH, IN 1964 HE CAME OUT WITH HIS MOST SCATHING REBUKE YET OF MODERN SOCIETY.

SUBMISSION IS THE TRUE THEME OF THIS, MARCUSE'S MOST INFLUENTIAL BOOK.

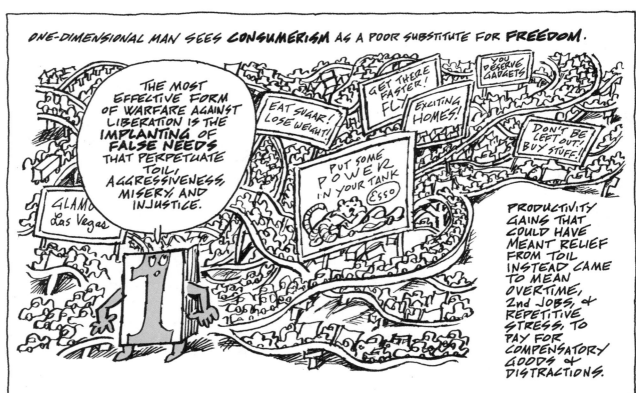

ONE-DIMENSIONAL MAN SEES **CONSUMERISM** AS A POOR SUBSTITUTE FOR **FREEDOM**.

SOME HAVE RIGHTLY CRITICIZED ONE-DIMENSIONAL MAN FOR EXAGGERATING THE DEGREE OF SOCIAL HARMONIZATION IN POST-WW2 AMERICA.

AN OVERRIDING INTEREST IN THE PRESERVATION OF THE STATUS QUO UNITES THE FORMER ANTAGONISTS.

CAPITAL & LABOR

I'M OK, YOU'RE OK

IF THE WORKER & HIS BOSS VISIT THE SAME RESORT & READ THE SAME NEWSPAPER, THIS INDICATES NOT THE DISAPPEARANCE OF CLASSES—

—BUT THAT THE NEEDS OF THE ESTABLISHMENT ARE SHARED BY THE UNDERLYING POPULATION.

CERTAINLY BY THE EARLY 1960s U.S. WORKERS HAD WON SIGNIFICANT GAINS, AND IF THEY WEREN'T EXACTLY READING THE SAME NEWSPAPERS AS THEIR EMPLOYERS—

WISE PUNDITS CALL FOR U.S. INTERVENTION

EAT LEADEN DEATH, SAVAGE REBELS!

—THEY WERE GETTING SIMILAR MESSAGES.

BUT SINCE THEN, 50+ YEARS OF CORPORATE REVENGE AGAINST LABOR SUGGEST THAT MARCUSE'S CHARACTERIZATION OF THE UNDERLYING PROBLEM WAS SPOT ON:

GONE

DONE

CLOSED

THE SURRENDER OF **THOUGHT, HOPE,** & **FEAR** TO THE DECISIONS OF THE POWERS THAT BE!

THE DYSTOPIA OF UNNECESSARY TOIL IS REPLACED IN *ONE-DIMENSIONAL MAN* BY A DYSTOPIA OF DISEMPOWERING LEISURE.

THE GARDEN OF EDEN

GIT!

THE EXPULSION

HUMANITY WANDERS THE EARTH, COMPELLED TO LIVE BY THE LABOR OF ITS THUMBS.

THE DECLINING PROPORTION OF HUMAN LABOR IN THE PRODUCTIVE PROCESS MEANS A DECLINE IN THE POLITICAL POWER OF THE OPPOSITION.

ONE-DIMENSIONAL MAN TURNED MARCUSE INTO A CAMPUS SUPERSTAR.

I HOPE HE TALKS ABOUT EROS & CIVILIZATION!

PLEASE! HE WILL TALK ABOUT ONE-DIMENSIONAL MAN!

CAPITALISM IS COLLAPSING & ALL YOU CAN THINK ABOUT IS YOUR DAMN ORGASM!

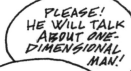
(CONVERSATION REPORTED IN A 1970 PLAYBOY ARTICLE)

THE BOOK WAS MORE POPULAR WITH STUDENTS THAN FACULTY.

ITS CLAIMS WERE EXPLICITLY AT ODDS WITH OPERATIONALISM & BEHAVIORISM, THE RULING IDEOLOGIES OF ACADEMIA AT THE TIME.

TROUBLESOME CONCEPTS LIKE **REASON** ARE BEING ELIMINATED TO JUSTIFY THE DEBUNKING OF THE MIND **BY THE INTELLECTUALS.**

RATS IN A MAZE

THIS IS ALL YE KNOW & ALL YE NEED TO KNOW!

SO THERE WASN'T ROOM FOR YOUR CHAPTER ON "TOLERANCE" IN *ONE-DIMENSIONAL MAN*, & YOU WANT TO BRING IT OUT SEPARATELY, WITH RELATED ESSAYS BY YOUR FRIENDS HERE.

WHAT SHOULD WE CALL IT?

BEACON PRESS

BARRINGTON MOORE

ROBERT PAUL WOLFF

HOW ABOUT "THE CRITIQUE OF PURE TOLERANCE"?

BUT HERBERT! I'M TRYING TO ESTABLISH MYSELF AS A KANT SCHOLAR! THIS WILL MAKE ME LOOK RIDICULOUS!

DON'T WORRY, ROBERT, NOBODY WILL READ IT.

OOPS! THE *CRITIQUE OF PURE TOLERANCE*, & ESPECIALLY MARCUSE'S CONTRIBUTION, "REPRESSIVE TOLERANCE," BECAME INFAMOUS.

HANDS OFF MY MAGNANIMOUS TOLERATION!

CRITIQUE OF PURE TOLERANCE

LIBERALS & CONSERVATIVES ALIKE USED IT—ARE STILL USING IT—TO DISCREDIT MARCUSE'S IDEAS.

TOLERANCE IS AN END IN ITSELF, BUT IT LOSES ITS MEANING IN A REPRESSIVE CULTURE.

TOLERANCE & FREE SPEECH WERE PROMOTED BY WRITERS LIKE JOHN STUART MILL BECAUSE THEY OPENED A PATH TO **TRUTH** & **LIBERATION**.

NOT BECAUSE HE THOUGHT ALL OPINIONS WERE EQUAL.

SLAVERY IS NONE OF YOUR BUSINESS

SLAVERY IS WRONG

MARCUSE CERTAINLY HAD HIS REASONS FOR SKEPTICISM ABOUT "PURE TOLERANCE."

THE SPEECHES OF THE FASCIST & NAZI LEADERS WERE THE IMMEDIATE PROLOGUE TO THE MASSACRE.

IF DEMOCRATIC TOLERANCE HAD BEEN WITHDRAWN WHEN THE NAZIS BEGAN THEIR CAMPAIGN, MANKIND MIGHT HAVE AVOIDED AUSCHWITZ & A WORLD WAR.

65

WHAT DO YOU DO WITH A WILDLY POPULAR TEACHER WHO ANNOYS THE DONORS & THE ACADEMIC BIG SHOTS? SHOW HIM THE DOOR.

IN 1965 INGE & HERBERT MOVED TO CALIFORNIA, WHERE THE NEW SAN DIEGO CAMPUS OF THE UNIVERSITY OF CALIFORNIA HAD OFFERED HIM A JOB.

RICKY SHEROVER & BILL LEISS FOLLOWED MARCUSE TO UCSD. ANGELA DAVIS, ON MARCUSE'S ADVICE, WENT TO GERMANY TO PURSUE A PhD WITH ADORNO.

IN FRANKFURT, DAVIS WAS ABLE TO EXPLORE THE GERMAN PHILOSOPHERS ON THEIR OWN TURF.

U.S. RAUS AUS VIETNAM

BUT THE VIETNAM WAR HAD ESCALATED, & THE ALMOST DAILY ANTI-IMPERIALIST STREET ACTIONS IN FRANKFURT & BERLIN WERE A DISTRACTION.

EVEN MORE UNSETTLING WERE REPORTS FROM THE BLACK STRUGGLE AT HOME.

YOUR DESIRE TO WORK DIRECTLY WITH RADICAL MOVEMENTS IS AKIN TO A MEDIA STUDIES SCHOLAR DECIDING TO BECOME A RADIO TECHNICIAN!

BLACK POWER

BY ANY MEANS NECESSARY

ADORNO

IN GERMANY, "IT WAS INCREASINGLY HARD TO FEEL A PART OF THE **COMING TO CONSCIOUSNESS** OF MY PEOPLE." —FROM DAVIS'S AUTOBIOGRAPHY

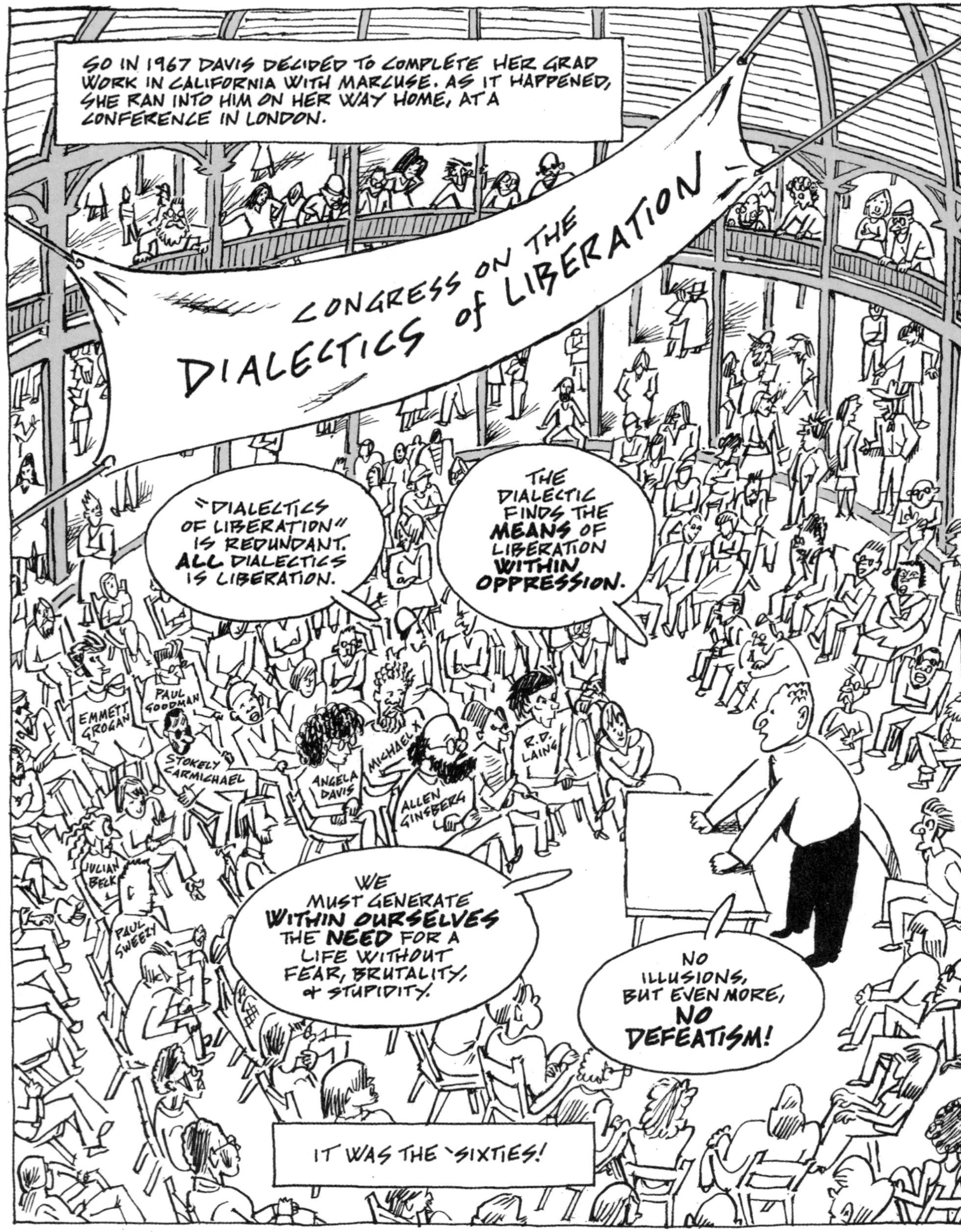
SO IN 1967 DAVIS DECIDED TO COMPLETE HER GRAD WORK IN CALIFORNIA WITH MARCUSE. AS IT HAPPENED, SHE RAN INTO HIM ON HER WAY HOME, AT A CONFERENCE IN LONDON.
CONGRESS ON THE DIALECTICS of LIBERATION
"DIALECTICS OF LIBERATION" IS REDUNDANT. ALL DIALECTICS IS LIBERATION.
THE DIALECTIC FINDS THE MEANS OF LIBERATION WITHIN OPPRESSION.
EMMETT GROGAN
PAUL GOODMAN
STOKELY CARMICHAEL
ANGELA DAVIS
MICHAEL X
ALLEN GINSBERG
R.D. LAING
JULIAN BECK
PAUL SWEEZY
WE MUST GENERATE WITHIN OURSELVES THE NEED FOR A LIFE WITHOUT FEAR, BRUTALITY, & STUPIDITY.
NO ILLUSIONS, BUT EVEN MORE, NO DEFEATISM!
IT WAS THE 'SIXTIES!

CHAPTER 6

THE RELUCTANT GURU

LATER IN 1967, MARCUSE WAS INTRODUCED TO AN ADORING CROWD IN BERLIN BY GERMAN RADICAL STUDENT LEADER RUDI DEUTSHKE.

M! M! M!

MAO!

MARX!

MARCUSE!

?

THE PROVOCATIVE ASSOCIATION OF MARCUSE'S NAME WITH THOSE OF KARL MARX & MAO ZEDONG CAUGHT THE ATTENTION OF A CONSERVATIVE NEWSPAPER BACK HOME.

SAN DIEGO UNION-TRIBUNE Editorials

COMMIE PROFESSOR SHOULD BE FIRED

STUDENTS SHOULD BE MORE POLITE

WE SHOULD GO BACK TO THE WAY THINGS WERE

NEGROES SHOULD BE MORE PATIENT

DAMN STRAIGHT!

(SAN DIEGO DURING THE VIETNAM WAR WAS A MILITARIZED ZONE AND—BY CALIFORNIA STANDARDS—A SOUTHERN CITY.)

LEADING POLITICIANS JUMPED ON THE BANDWAGON.

CALIFORNIA GOVERNOR RONALD REAGAN DEMANDED (& EVENTUALLY ACHIEVED) MARCUSE'S EJECTION FROM THE UCSD PHILOSOPHY DEPARTMENT.

YOU HAVE A VERY EXTREME PROFESSOR SUCH AS MARCUSE LITERALLY POISONING A LOT OF YOUNG LIVES WITH SOME OF THE MOST IRRESPONSIBLE DRIVEL I'VE EVER READ. WE SHOULD FOCUS MORE ON TRAINING THESE YOUNG PEOPLE TO BE PRODUCTIVE CITIZENS & NOT TO DISSECT & EXAMINE THE MOTIVES OF HUMAN BEINGS.

VICE PRESIDENT SPIRO AGNEW

AND SOME LEADING ACTORS AS WELL.

LIBERALS SEEM TO BE QUITE WILLING TO HAVE COMMUNISTS TEACHING THEIR KIDS AT SCHOOL.

MARCUSE HAS BECOME A HERO TO AN ARTICULATE CLIQUE.

(DID HE SAY "ARTICULATE"?)

(!)

(FROM A 1971 PLAYBOY INTERVIEW WITH JOHN WAYNE)

GUESS WHAT CAME IN THE MAIL TODAY?

Marcuse—
You are a very dirty Communist dog. We give you 72 hours to live in the United States. 72 hours, Marcuse, and we kill you.
—Ku Klux Klan

PROFESSOR, I DON'T REMEMBER SEEING THOSE HOLES BEFORE.

OH, YES, WELL, IT SEEMS SOMEBODY EMPTIED A MAGAZINE INTO OUR GARAGE DOOR LAST NIGHT.

MARCUSE'S GRAD STUDENTS BEGAN ACCOMPANYING HIM FROM HOME TO CAMPUS & BACK.

IN YOUR SEMINAR LAST WEEK WE SPENT THE WHOLE TIME ON A SINGLE PAGE OF HEGEL'S DOCTRINE OF ESSENCE.

ISN'T THE PACE A LITTLE SLOW HERE?

IN FREIBURG, HEIDEGGER HAD US SPEND AN ENTIRE SEMESTER ON THE FIRST PAGE OF ARISTOTLE'S METAPHYSICS.

AND WE HAD TO READ IT IN THE ORIGINAL GREEK.

DO YOU KNOW HOW TO USE THAT THING?

FOR A BRIEF TIME, HERBERT & INGE WENT INTO HIDING.

HE NEEDED A BREAK ANYWAY.

IT'S HARD WORK POISONING YOUNG LIVES.

WHERE DID THIS IDEA OF CORRUPTING THE YOUNG COME FROM?

SOME PROFS HAD RADICAL VIEWS IN THOSE DAYS BUT VERY FEW SUPPORTED THE NEW LEFT'S MILITANT ACTIVISM.

(I'M HAPPY TO SAY THAT MY FATHER WAS ONE OF THE FEW. HE GOT HIMSELF ARRESTED AT AN ANTI-WAR SIT-IN AT HIS UNIVERSITY.)

PROFESSOR THORKELSON! WHY ARE YOU LEADING THE STUDENTS ASTRAY?

HAW HAW HAW

LEADING THEM ASTRAY?

I'M JUST RACING TO CATCH UP!

FOR THE MOST PART, WITCH HUNTS HAD SILENCED THE RADICALS OF THE ANTI-FASCIST GENERATION.

WE HAD TO CLEANSE OUR INSTITUTIONS OF LEFTIST TRAITORS IN ORDER TO ASSUME LEADERSHIP OF THE FREE WORLD.

EMPIRE

"FREE" IN WHAT SENSE?

GUATEMALA
ALGERIA
IRAN
CONGO
INDOCHINA

WE WHO CAME OF AGE IN THE 1960s HAD TO FIGURE OUT A LOT OF THINGS FOR OURSELVES.

WE GOT SOME HELP FROM A LEADING SOCIALIST, WHOSE 1962 BESTSELLER "DISCOVERED POVERTY."

MICHAEL HARRINGTON — The Other America

POVERTY IS DEEPLY BUILT INTO THE ECONOMIC MECHANISMS OF SOCIETY.

TO ABOLISH IT WOULD REQUIRE CONFLICT & NOT SIMPLY CONSENSUS.

MICHAEL HARRINGTON WAS CHAIR OF THE LEAGUE FOR INDUSTRIAL DEMOCRACY, WHOSE YOUTH GROUP MORPHED INTO THE PREEMINENT "NEW LEFT" ORGANIZATION, STUDENTS FOR A DEMOCRATIC SOCIETY (SDS).

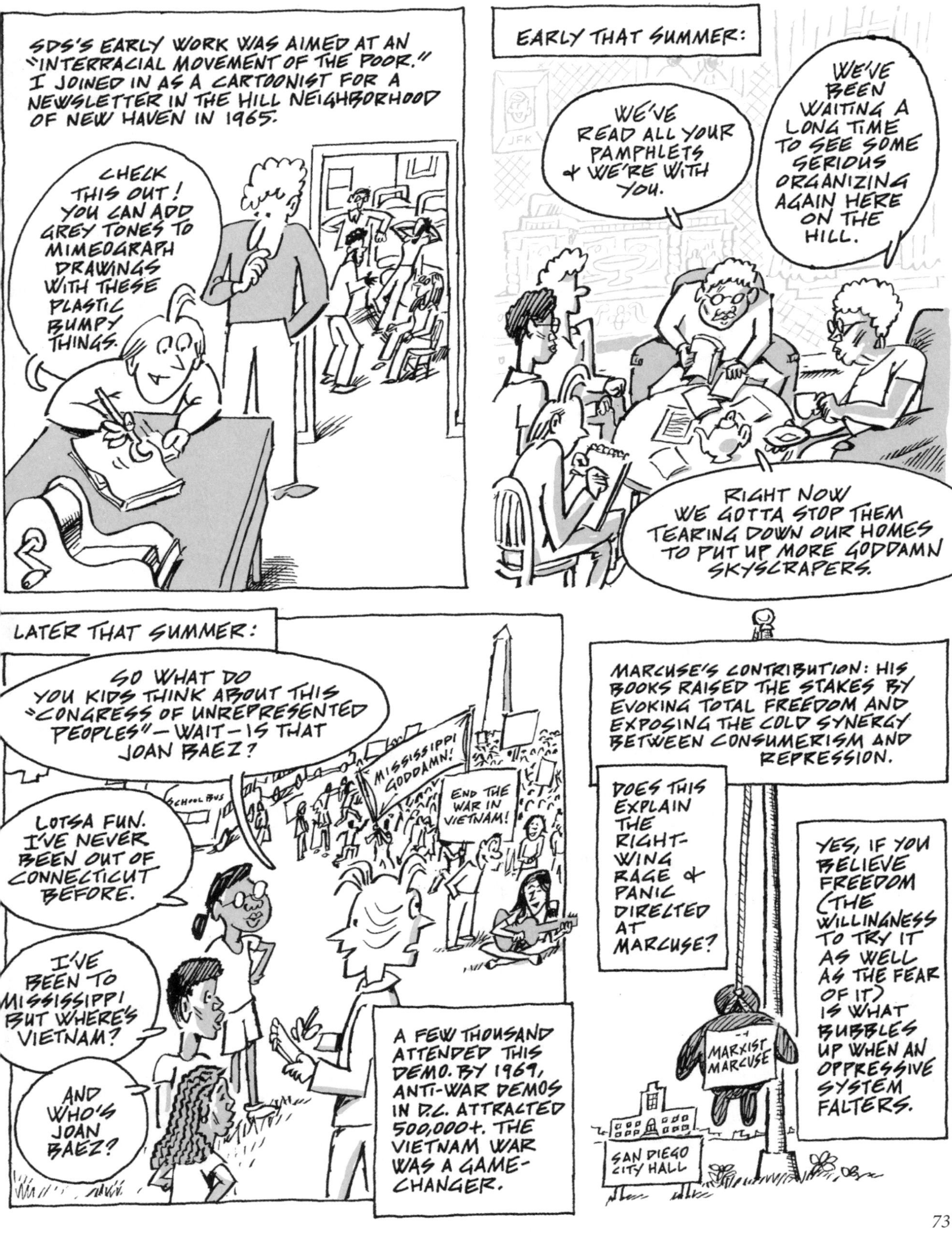
SDS'S EARLY WORK WAS AIMED AT AN "INTERRACIAL MOVEMENT OF THE POOR." I JOINED IN AS A CARTOONIST FOR A NEWSLETTER IN THE HILL NEIGHBORHOOD OF NEW HAVEN IN 1965.
CHECK THIS OUT! YOU CAN ADD GREY TONES TO MIMEOGRAPH DRAWINGS WITH THESE PLASTIC BUMPY THINGS.
EARLY THAT SUMMER:
JFK
WE'VE READ ALL YOUR PAMPHLETS & WE'RE WITH YOU.
WE'VE BEEN WAITING A LONG TIME TO SEE SOME SERIOUS ORGANIZING AGAIN HERE ON THE HILL.
RIGHT NOW WE GOTTA STOP THEM TEARING DOWN OUR HOMES TO PUT UP MORE GODDAMN SKYSCRAPERS.
LATER THAT SUMMER:
SO WHAT DO YOU KIDS THINK ABOUT THIS "CONGRESS OF UNREPRESENTED PEOPLES"— WAIT— IS THAT JOAN BAEZ?
SCHOOL BUS
MISSISSIPPI GODDAMN!
END THE WAR IN VIETNAM!
LOTSA FUN. I'VE NEVER BEEN OUT OF CONNECTICUT BEFORE.
I'VE BEEN TO MISSISSIPPI BUT WHERE'S VIETNAM?
AND WHO'S JOAN BAEZ?
A FEW THOUSAND ATTENDED THIS DEMO. BY 1969, ANTI-WAR DEMOS IN D.C. ATTRACTED 500,000+. THE VIETNAM WAR WAS A GAME-CHANGER.
MARCUSE'S CONTRIBUTION: HIS BOOKS RAISED THE STAKES BY EVOKING TOTAL FREEDOM AND EXPOSING THE COLD SYNERGY BETWEEN CONSUMERISM AND REPRESSION.
DOES THIS EXPLAIN THE RIGHT-WING RAGE & PANIC DIRECTED AT MARCUSE?
YES, IF YOU BELIEVE FREEDOM (THE WILLINGNESS TO TRY IT AS WELL AS THE FEAR OF IT) IS WHAT BUBBLES UP WHEN AN OPPRESSIVE SYSTEM FALTERS.
MARXIST MARCUSE
SAN DIEGO CITY HALL

THE WILLINGNESS TO **TRY FREEDOM** HAD MANY SOURCES, BUT IT ALSO CAME OUT OF **NOWHERE**, WHICH IS THE LITERAL MEANING OF THE WORD "UTOPIA."

"HA HA"

"HA"

"HA HA"

"HA"

"HA HA HA"

"HA HA HA"

"HA"

EVERYONE KNOWS THIS IS NOWHERE.

AMERICA'S POST-WW2 UTOPIA WAS THE LILY-WHITE SUBURB, WITH ITS HOMOGENEOUS & (MOSTLY) INSIPID POP CULTURE.

LONG BEFORE WAR & REBELLION SHATTERED THE COLD WAR **POLITICAL** CONSENSUS—

—THE LONGING FOR AUTHENTIC **CULTURE** GAVE RISE TO THE FOLK SONG MOVEMENT.

JOAN BAEZ WAS CONSIDERED A FOLKSINGER ALTHOUGH HER VOCAL STYLE WAS SOPHISTICATED BEL CANTO.

REVEREND GARY DAVIS

DAVE VAN RONK

WOODY GUTHRIE

MEMPHIS MINNIE

BOB DYLAN

JANIS JOPLIN

BUT REBELS IN THE FOLK SCENE CALLED FOR THE ROUGH VOCALIZING OF HILLBILLY STRING BANDS, COUNTRY BLUES, AND—PREVIOUSLY TABOO AMONG FOLKIES—**ROCK n ROLL!**

1960s ROCK MUSIC, & THE COUNTERCULTURE OF WHICH IT WAS AN ESSENTIAL PART, DREAMED ALONG WITH MARCUSE OF AN **ANTI-UTOPIA**—

—A FREE LIFE THAT WAS **NOT** NOWHERE BECAUSE IT FELT LIKE IT WAS WITHIN OUR REACH.

AND SOON THE NEWS SPREAD!

HOW FAR YOU GOIN'? I'LL TAKE YOU THERE.

THE WORLD IS CHANGING, DON'T YOU THINK?

THE OLD PEOPLE WORRY EVERY DAY, & TELL YOU TO KEEP YOUR HEAD DOWN.

BUT WE KNOW IT'S NOT LIKE THAT.

EASY DOES IT! GO FOR IT!

RIGHT?

YOU HOLD THE KEY TO LOVE AND FEAR ALL IN YOUR TREMBLING HAND ♪

NOT ALL MUSICAL PIONEERS IN THE 1960s WERE "POLITICAL." BUT THOSE WHO WERE DID NOT PULL THEIR PUNCHES.

(THIS BEING A COMIC, I CAN ONLY REFERENCE LYRICS, NOT SOUNDS.)

WE INSIST! MAX ROACH'S FREEDOM NOW SUITE

FEATURING ABBEY LINCOLN, COLEMAN HAWKINS, † OLATUNJI

♪ AIN'T BUT ♪ ONE THING ON MY MIND; DRIVA MAN & QUITTIN' TIME

JIMI HENDRIX BAND OF GYPSYS

EVIL MAN MAKE YOU KILL ME, EVEN THOUGH ♪ WE'RE ONLY FAMILIES APART

imagine john lennon

IMAGINE NO POSSESSIONS—I WONDER ♪ IF YOU CAN

SADLY, MOST OF THIS CREATIVITY SAILED OVER THE HEADS OF THE RIGIDLY HIGHBROW CRITICAL THEORISTS.

NO MATTER. IN HIS 1970 BOOK, AN *ESSAY ON LIBERATION,* MARCUSE CLEARLY HAS HIS FINGER ON THE PULSE OF THE NEW CULTURE.

FREEDOM WILL BE THE ENVIRONMENT OF AN ORGANISM THAT IS NO LONGER CAPABLE OF ADAPTING TO THE **COMPETITIVE PERFORMANCES** REQUIRED FOR WELL-BEING UNDER DOMINATION.

DID I COLONIZE, KIDNAP, ENSLAVE, & NEGLECT MYSELF & THEN, BEING REDUCED TO NOTHING, INVENT A COMPETITIVE ECONOMY, KNOWING THAT **I** *CANNOT COMPETE?* ＊

＊ FROM GEORGE JACKSON'S PRISON LETTERS— MORE ABOUT GEORGE JACKSON IN A MOMENT.

IN FACT, AN *ESSAY ON LIBERATION* EXPRESSES A SURPRISING OPENNESS TO THE YOUNG REBELS' ENTHUSIASM FOR POPULAR CULTURE.

THE PIANO WITH THE JAZZ PLAYER STOOD WELL BETWEEN THE BARRICADES.

JAZZ'S "MODERNITY" IS POLARIZED BETWEEN **SOULLESSNESS** & LICENTIOUS DECADENCE!

ADORNO

"DON'T SHOOT THE PIANO PLAYER"

LIKE THE MAY 1968 BARRICADES IN PARIS, AN *ESSAY ON LIBERATION* SHOOK UP MARXISM.

MARX'S INTERNATIONAL WORKERS' ASSOCIATION WAS THE LAST ATTEMPT TO REALIZE THE SOLIDARITY OF THE SPECIES.

BUT THE MARXIAN EXAMPLE OF FREE INDIVIDUALS HUNTING, FISHING, CRITICIZING, ETC., HAS AN EMBARRASINGLY RIDICULOUS SOUND BECAUSE MARX REJECTS THE IDEA THAT WORK CAN BECOME PLAY.

YOU'RE AIMING THAT GUN THE WRONG WAY.

I ACCEPT YOUR CRITICISM.

AT THE SAME TIME, THANKS TO THE BARRICADES, HE WAS ABLE TO RECLAIM MARX'S OPTIMISM.

TODAY THE POSSIBILITY OF FREEDOM **WITHIN** THE REALM OF NECESSITY—

POWER TO THE IMAGINATION!

ENJOY WITHOUT CHAINS!

WORKERS OF THE WORLD HAVE FUN!

—IS THE **NEW IDEA** OF THE REBELLION IN FRANCE.

MARCUSE WAS ACTUALLY IN PARIS FOR A UNESCO CONFERENCE WHEN THE 1968 REBELLION WAS GATHERING STEAM.

IT'S HIM!

PROFESSOR, YOU HAVE BEEN DESCRIBED IN THE PRESS AS THE GURU OF THE NEW LEFT.

MY HERO!

THE WHAT? I'M THE WHAT?

HE WAS INVITED TO ADDRESS STUDENTS WHO HAD OCCUPIED THE ÉCOLE DES BEAUX ARTS.

I GREET YOU IN THE NAME OF THE AMERICAN MOVEMENT.

AND I SALUTE YOU FOR REJECTING CONSUMERISM.

SAVE THESE. THEY'LL BE VALUABLE SOME DAY.

THERE WAS INSPIRATION CLOSER TO HOME AS WELL.

ERICA SHEROVER

LOWELL BERGMAN

BILL LEISS

ANDREW FEENBERG

TONIGHT: SONORA ACTIVISTS SPEAK ON CLASS STRUGGLE + SANCTUARY

GEORGE KATSIAFICAS

DAVID INGRAM

EVEN BEFORE ANGELA DAVIS'S RETURN FROM GERMANY, THE CIRCLE OF YOUNG ACTIVISTS STUDYING WITH MARCUSE, & THEIR SCENE DOWN THE BEACH FROM UCSD'S LA JOLLA CAMPUS, ALLOWED MARCUSE TO BECOME A STUDENT AGAIN.

THE STUDENT MOVEMENT DOESN'T NEED A FATHER.

THE "RED HOUSE"

MARCUSE HAD HIS CRITICISMS OF THE SCENE, OF COURSE.

Nelson Rockefeller sleeps better at night, knowing our anti-CIA coalition has disbanded.

I ENJOY READING YOUR UNDERGROUND PAPER—

BUT DO YOU KNOW HOW TO SAY "MEGALOMANIA"?

76

ASKED BY BILL LEISS & ANDREW FEENBERG TO WRITE SOMETHING FOR ANOTHER RADICAL STUDENT PERIODICAL, MARCUSE OFFERED:

"The Individual in the Great Society"

IN 1964, PRES. LYNDON JOHNSON HAD CALLED FOR PROGRAMS ATTACKING POVERTY & DISCRIMINATION, & EXPANDING EDUCATION & HEALTH CARE.

WITH YOUR COURAGE & COMPASSION, WE WILL BUILD A **GREAT SOCIETY**.

A SOCIETY WHERE NO CHILD WILL GO UNFED, NO YOUNGSTER UNSCHOOLED.

THE GREAT SOCIETY IS NOT A SAFE HARBOR, A RESTING PLACE.

IT BECKONS US TO A DESTINY WHERE THE MEANING OF OUR LIVES MATCHES THE MARVELOUS PRODUCTS OF OUR LABOR!

THE GREAT SOCIETY INITIATIVE GAVE US HEAD START & MEDICARE, BUT ITS CENTERPIECE—THE "WAR ON POVERTY"—DID NOT END WELL.

MARCUSE'S CRITIQUE:

SHOULDN'T IT BE THE OTHER WAY AROUND? FREE INDIVIDUALS DECIDE WHAT THEIR LIVES MEAN, & DETERMINE THE PRODUCTS OF THEIR LABOR ACCORDINGLY?

I WISH I COULD MAKE A SHIRT THAT WOULD NEVER WEAR OUT.

WATCH YOUR MOUTH!

CHEAP THREAD

SHODDY FABRIC

AND WHAT'S WRONG WITH A "SAFE HARBOR," WHERE LIFE IS NO LONGER SPENT IN THE STRUGGLE FOR EXISTENCE?

STAY THE COURSE!

AN EFFECTIVE WAR ON POVERTY WOULD NOT **INCREASE** PRODUCTIVITY BUT **REDIRECT** IT, AWAY FROM WASTE & ARMAMENTS.

BUT IN OUR WORLD, THE TRANSFER OF POWER FROM THE INDIVIDUAL TO THE APPARATUS CREATES A SURPLUS OF AGGRESSION WHICH IS RELEASED IN A WAR **AGAINST** THE POOR.

I HAVE LIVED THROUGH 2 WORLD WARS—

BUT I CANNOT REMEMBER ANY SUCH BRAZEN ADVERTISEMENTS OF SLAUGHTER.

MARINES KILL 165

136 VIETCONG KILLED

MORE THAN 240 REDS SLAIN

LBJ'S WAR ON POVERTY COLLAPSED BEFORE THE WAR IN VIETNAM.

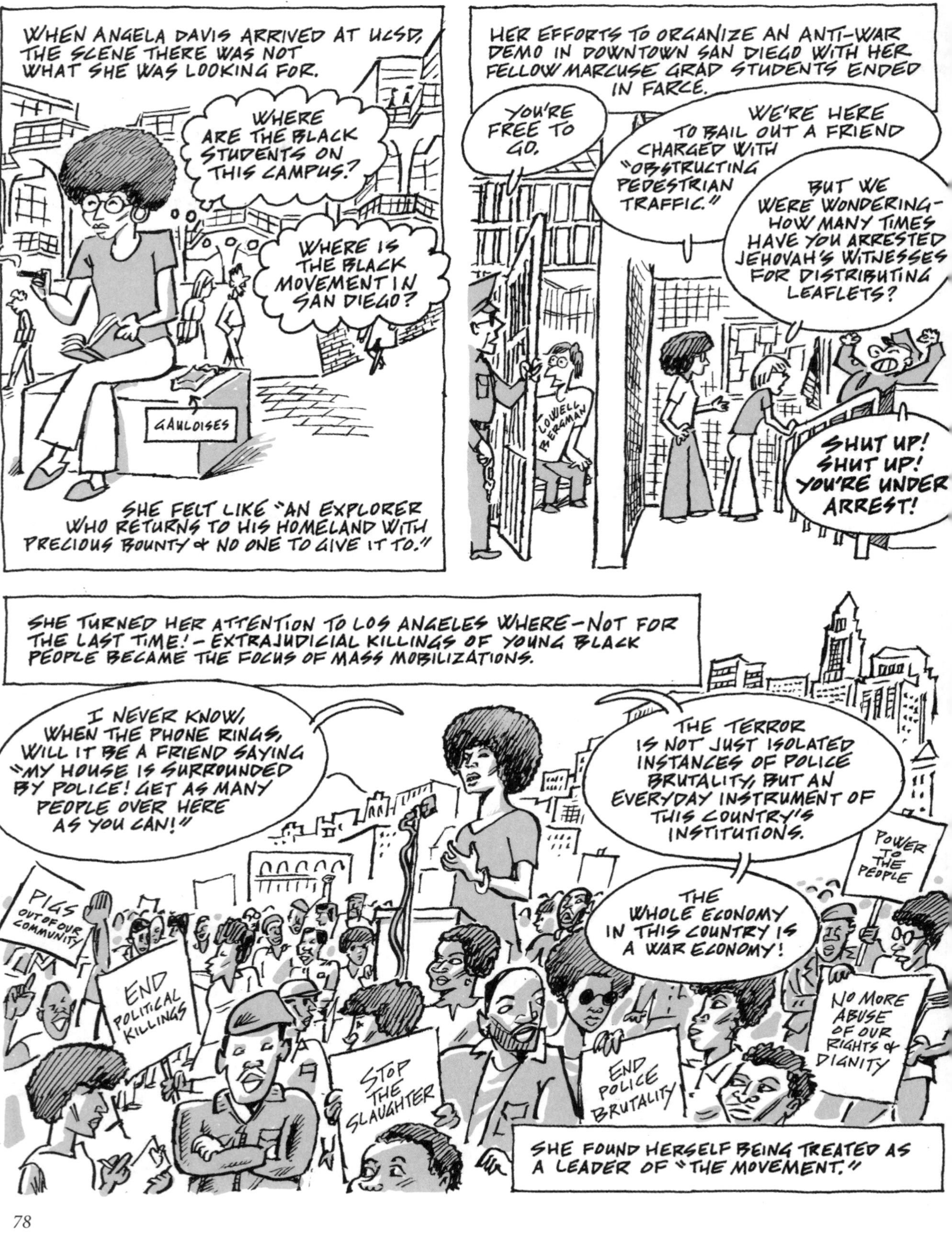
WHEN ANGELA DAVIS ARRIVED AT UCSD, THE SCENE THERE WAS NOT WHAT SHE WAS LOOKING FOR.
WHERE ARE THE BLACK STUDENTS ON THIS CAMPUS?
WHERE IS THE BLACK MOVEMENT IN SAN DIEGO?
GAULOISES
SHE FELT LIKE "AN EXPLORER WHO RETURNS TO HIS HOMELAND WITH PRECIOUS BOUNTY & NO ONE TO GIVE IT TO."
HER EFFORTS TO ORGANIZE AN ANTI-WAR DEMO IN DOWNTOWN SAN DIEGO WITH HER FELLOW MARCUSE GRAD STUDENTS ENDED IN FARCE.
YOU'RE FREE TO GO.
WE'RE HERE TO BAIL OUT A FRIEND CHARGED WITH "OBSTRUCTING PEDESTRIAN TRAFFIC."
BUT WE WERE WONDERING- HOW MANY TIMES HAVE YOU ARRESTED JEHOVAH'S WITNESSES FOR DISTRIBUTING LEAFLETS?
LOWELL BERGMAN
SHUT UP! SHUT UP! YOU'RE UNDER ARREST!
SHE TURNED HER ATTENTION TO LOS ANGELES WHERE—NOT FOR THE LAST TIME!—EXTRAJUDICIAL KILLINGS OF YOUNG BLACK PEOPLE BECAME THE FOCUS OF MASS MOBILIZATIONS.
I NEVER KNOW, WHEN THE PHONE RINGS, WILL IT BE A FRIEND SAYING "MY HOUSE IS SURROUNDED BY POLICE! GET AS MANY PEOPLE OVER HERE AS YOU CAN!"
THE TERROR IS NOT JUST ISOLATED INSTANCES OF POLICE BRUTALITY, BUT AN EVERYDAY INSTRUMENT OF THIS COUNTRY'S INSTITUTIONS.
THE WHOLE ECONOMY IN THIS COUNTRY IS A WAR ECONOMY!
POWER TO THE PEOPLE
PIGS OUT OF OUR COMMUNITY
END POLITICAL KILLINGS
STOP THE SLAUGHTER
END POLICE BRUTALITY
NO MORE ABUSE OF OUR RIGHTS & DIGNITY
SHE FOUND HERSELF BEING TREATED AS A LEADER OF "THE MOVEMENT."

SHE BRIEFLY JOINED THE BLACK PANTHER PARTY FOR SELF DEFENSE, IN SOLIDARITY WITH THEIR RESISTANCE TO POLICE BRUTALITY, BUT QUIT DUE TO PARTY INFIGHTING.

> I SUPPOSE I SHOULD COLLECT MY BOOKS & GET ON BACK TO SCHOOL.

ZORA NEALE HURSTON — THEIR EYES WERE WATCHING GOD

C.L.R. JAMES — THE BLACK JACOBINS

DUBOIS — THE SOULS OF BLACK FOLK

FANON — THE WRETCHED OF THE EARTH

THE AUTOBIOGRAPHY OF MALCOLM X

BACK IN SAN DIEGO, DAVIS HELPED ORGANIZE UCSD'S BLACK & CHICANO STUDENTS TO DEMAND THE CREATION OF A "LUMUMBA-ZAPATA COLLEGE."

THE NEW COLLEGE WITHIN THE UNIVERSITY WOULD HONOR CONGOLESE & MEXICAN REVOLUTIONARY MARTYRS, AND MAKE THE CAMPUS MORE WELCOMING TO STUDENTS OF COLOR.

BUT THE DEMAND FOR A NEW COLLEGE WAS NOT SIMPLY ABOUT RECRUITING BLACK & CHICANO STUDENTS.

> STUDENTS WILL LEARN ABOUT THE CRUCIAL ROLE PLAYED BY COLONIALISM, SLAVERY, & GENOCIDE IN THE DEVELOPMENT OF U.S. CAPITALISM.

> COULDN'T THEY JUST TALK ABOUT MINORITIES WHO INVENTED THINGS?

> I THINK THEY WANT HISTORY THEY CAN USE.

THESE PROPOSALS DID NOT THRILL THE UCSD ADMINISTRATION! NEGOTIATIONS DRAGGED ON FOR A YEAR.

FINALLY, JUST AS THE DESPERATE STUDENTS WERE OCCUPYING THE REGISTRAR'S OFFICE, THEY LEARNED THE FACULTY SENATE HAD AGREED TO THEIR BASIC DEMANDS.

> THIS ISN'T THE WAY I USUALLY COME IN HERE.

MARCUSE PLAYED A CRUCIAL ROLE IN PERSUADING THE FACULTY, & HE WAS THE FIRST ONE THROUGH THE DOOR DURING THE BRIEF OCCUPATION.

(AND HE PAID TO HAVE THE DOOR REPLACED.)

MARCUSE'S WILLINGNESS TO STEP UP WHEN NEEDED HAD A LOT TO DO WITH INGE.

UCSD WANTS TO GET RID OF DAY CARE FOR ITS HISPANIC EMPLOYEES.

WE MUST DO SOMETHING ABOUT THIS!

UNLIKE HERBERT SHE CAME FROM AN ACTIVIST FAMILY IN GERMANY, WHICH GAVE HER A PRAGMATIC & PROACTIVE APPROACH TO POLITICS.

(SHE WAS LESS OBLIGING WHEN IT CAME TO INQUIRIES FROM THE MEDIA.)

IS PROFESSOR MARCUSE REALLY TRYING TO DESTROY WESTERN CIVILIZATION?

IF PEOPLE WANT TO KNOW WHAT HE HAS TO SAY, THEY HAVE TO READ HIS BOOKS.

MEDIA INQUIRIES INVARIABLY FOCUSED ON MARCUSE'S SUPPOSED ADVOCACY OF VIOLENCE & PRIVATION, AS IN THIS INTERVIEW WITH A FRENCH JOURNALIST:

DO YOU BELIEVE IN THE POSSIBILITY OF REVOLUTION IN THE UNITED STATES?

ABSOLUTELY NOT. NOT AT ALL.

WHY NOT?

BECAUSE THERE IS NO COLLABORATION BETWEEN THE STUDENTS & WORKERS, NOT EVEN AT THE LEVEL THAT OCCURRED IN FRANCE IN MAY. AND I CANNOT IMAGINE A REVOLUTION WITHOUT THE WORKING CLASS.

THE FRENCH VOTING PUBLIC SEEMS TO HAVE BEEN FRIGHTENED, NOT INSPIRED, BY THE MAY 1968 EVENTS.

WELL, WE MUST FIGHT THAT FEAR.

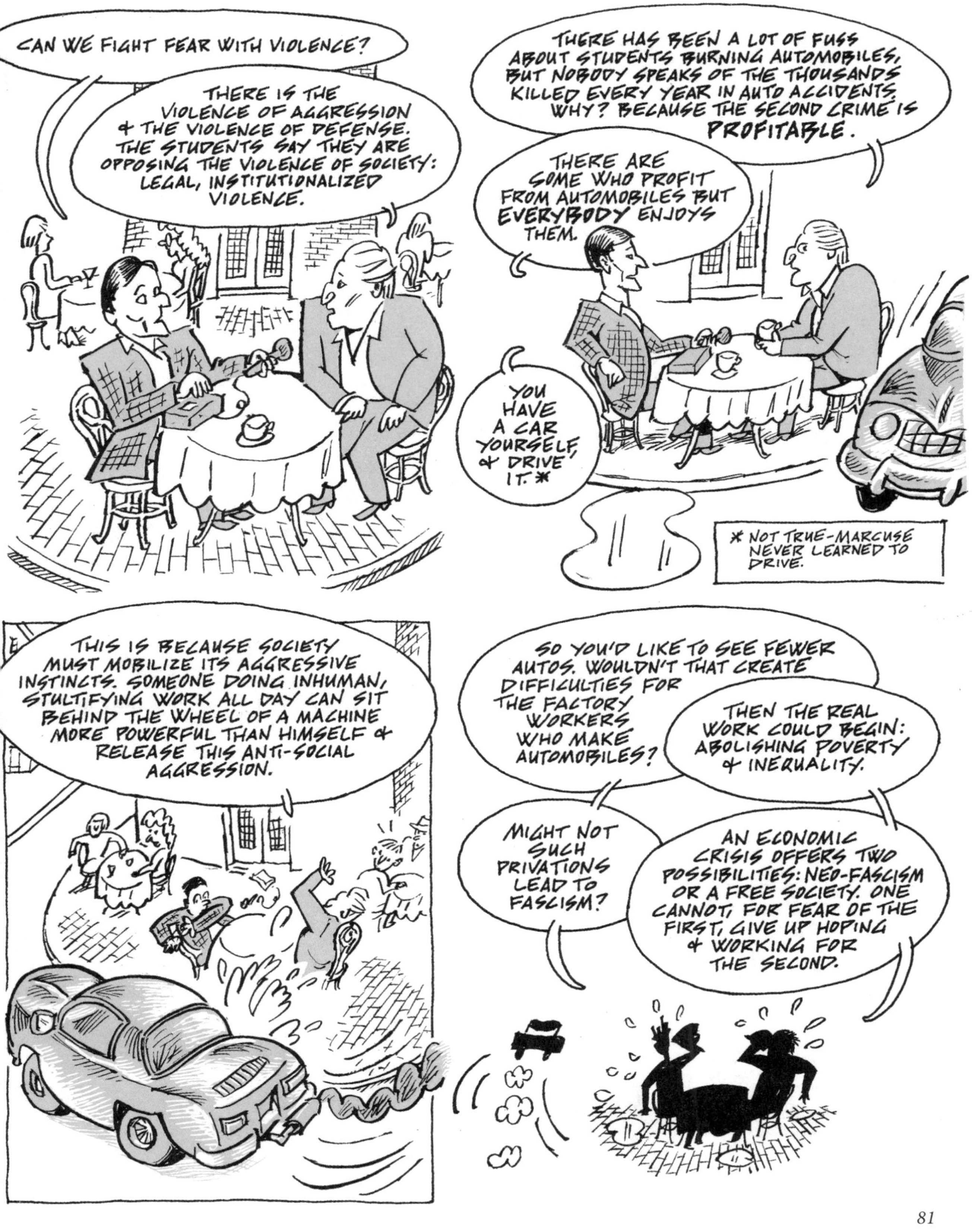
CAN WE FIGHT FEAR WITH VIOLENCE?
THERE IS THE VIOLENCE OF AGGRESSION & THE VIOLENCE OF DEFENSE. THE STUDENTS SAY THEY ARE OPPOSING THE VIOLENCE OF SOCIETY: LEGAL, INSTITUTIONALIZED VIOLENCE.
THERE HAS BEEN A LOT OF FUSS ABOUT STUDENTS BURNING AUTOMOBILES, BUT NOBODY SPEAKS OF THE THOUSANDS KILLED EVERY YEAR IN AUTO ACCIDENTS. WHY? BECAUSE THE SECOND CRIME IS PROFITABLE.
THERE ARE SOME WHO PROFIT FROM AUTOMOBILES BUT EVERYBODY ENJOYS THEM.
YOU HAVE A CAR YOURSELF, & DRIVE IT.*
* NOT TRUE-MARCUSE NEVER LEARNED TO DRIVE.
THIS IS BECAUSE SOCIETY MUST MOBILIZE ITS AGGRESSIVE INSTINCTS. SOMEONE DOING INHUMAN, STULTIFYING WORK ALL DAY CAN SIT BEHIND THE WHEEL OF A MACHINE MORE POWERFUL THAN HIMSELF & RELEASE THIS ANTI-SOCIAL AGGRESSION.
SO YOU'D LIKE TO SEE FEWER AUTOS. WOULDN'T THAT CREATE DIFFICULTIES FOR THE FACTORY WORKERS WHO MAKE AUTOMOBILES?
THEN THE REAL WORK COULD BEGIN: ABOLISHING POVERTY & INEQUALITY.
MIGHT NOT SUCH PRIVATIONS LEAD TO FASCISM?
AN ECONOMIC CRISIS OFFERS TWO POSSIBILITIES: NEO-FASCISM OR A FREE SOCIETY. ONE CANNOT, FOR FEAR OF THE FIRST, GIVE UP HOPING & WORKING FOR THE SECOND.

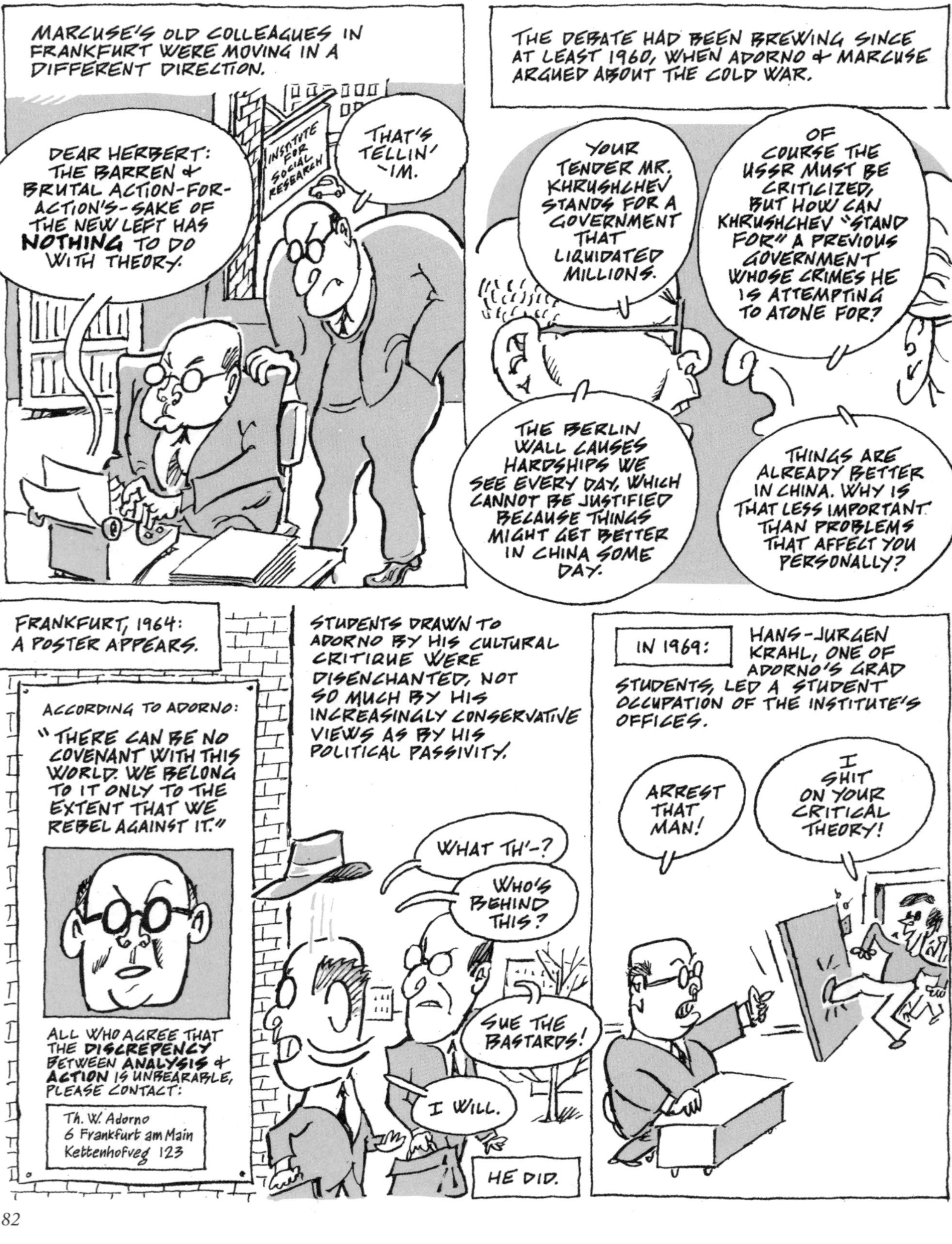
MARCUSE'S OLD COLLEAGUES IN FRANKFURT WERE MOVING IN A DIFFERENT DIRECTION.
INSTITUTE FOR SOCIAL RESEARCH
DEAR HERBERT: THE BARREN & BRUTAL ACTION-FOR-ACTION'S-SAKE OF THE NEW LEFT HAS **NOTHING** TO DO WITH THEORY.
THAT'S TELLIN' 'IM.
THE DEBATE HAD BEEN BREWING SINCE AT LEAST 1960, WHEN ADORNO & MARCUSE ARGUED ABOUT THE COLD WAR.
YOUR TENDER MR. KHRUSHCHEV STANDS FOR A GOVERNMENT THAT LIQUIDATED MILLIONS.
OF COURSE THE USSR MUST BE CRITICIZED, BUT HOW CAN KHRUSHCHEV "STAND FOR" A PREVIOUS GOVERNMENT WHOSE CRIMES HE IS ATTEMPTING TO ATONE FOR?
THE BERLIN WALL CAUSES HARDSHIPS WE SEE EVERY DAY, WHICH CANNOT BE JUSTIFIED BECAUSE THINGS MIGHT GET BETTER IN CHINA SOME DAY.
THINGS ARE ALREADY BETTER IN CHINA. WHY IS THAT LESS IMPORTANT THAN PROBLEMS THAT AFFECT YOU PERSONALLY?
FRANKFURT, 1964: A POSTER APPEARS.
ACCORDING TO ADORNO:
"THERE CAN BE NO COVENANT WITH THIS WORLD. WE BELONG TO IT ONLY TO THE EXTENT THAT WE REBEL AGAINST IT."
ALL WHO AGREE THAT THE **DISCREPENCY** BETWEEN **ANALYSIS & ACTION** IS UNBEARABLE, PLEASE CONTACT:
Th. W. Adorno
6 Frankfurt am Main
Kettenhofveg 123
STUDENTS DRAWN TO ADORNO BY HIS CULTURAL CRITIQUE WERE DISENCHANTED, NOT SO MUCH BY HIS INCREASINGLY CONSERVATIVE VIEWS AS BY HIS POLITICAL PASSIVITY.
WHAT TH'-?
WHO'S BEHIND THIS?
SUE THE BASTARDS!
I WILL.
HE DID.
IN 1969:
HANS-JURGEN KRAHL, ONE OF ADORNO'S GRAD STUDENTS, LED A STUDENT OCCUPATION OF THE INSTITUTE'S OFFICES.
ARREST THAT MAN!
I SHIT ON YOUR CRITICAL THEORY!

HIGHER EDUCATION WAS MORE PATERNALISTIC IN GERMANY THAN IN THE UNITED STATES, & GERMAN STUDENTS WERE CORRESPONDINGLY HARDER ON THEIR DADDY-PROFESSORS.

MARCUSE TO ADORNO:

I AM WILLING TO COME TO TERMS WITH PATRICIDE.

ADORNO WAS NOT WILLING. THE ANIMOSITY BETWEEN HIM & HIS RADICAL STUDENTS ESCALATED INTO A SERIES OF CLASSROOM CONFRONTATIONS.

I GOT YOUR DIALECTICS RIGHT HERE!

IN APRIL 1969, FEMALE STUDENTS INTERRUPTED HIS "INTRODUCTION TO DIALECTICS" LECTURE BY BARING THEIR BREASTS & SHOWERING HIM WITH ROSES & TULIPS.

IN WHAT WAS TO BE THE LAST YEAR OF HIS LIFE, ADORNO'S WILLINGNESS TO USE THE COURTS & POLICE AGAINST REBEL STUDENTS LED TO A FIERCE DEBATE BETWEEN HIMSELF & MARCUSE.

5 April 1969

Dear Teddy,

This is painful to write but-- isn't our cause better taken up by the students than by the police?

I would despair if I (we) were on the side of a world that supports mass murder in Vietnam, that turns any realm beyond its repressive power into hell.

I am happy we will meet soon. The lake country? Zurich? Our love to you & Gretel.

Herbert

3 May 1969

Dear Herbert,

You have formed an opinion from 6000 miles away, But I have to look out for the interests of the Institute-- our old Institute, Herbert.

You are deluding yourself about Vietnam if you do not also protest the unspeakable Chinese-style tortures that the Vietcong carry out constantly.

Zermatt would be the best place to meet. Fond regards to you & Inge.

Theodor

4 June 1969

No, Teddy, it is not our old Institute. Our theory had political content, that now demands we condemn U.S. imperialism. To say one cannot do so without condemning those who fight against this hell, by whatever means they can, seems inhuman.

We need to talk. Come to Zurich! Warm greetings to both of you.

Herbert

19 June 1969

The crux of the matter is that you think praxis is not blocked today. I disagree. The German students have not the tiniest prospect of effecting a social intervention but they _can_ inflame Germany's undiminished fascist potential. Can't you come to Zermatt, where I seek wretchedly to recuperate?

THE FINAL MESSAGES BETWEEN ADORNO & MARCUSE WERE MORE CONCILIATORY.

My discussions with European students show the self-promoting provocateurs to be fully isolated from the movement.

But why did Max say in an interview that "your" critical theory (as if I had no part in it) was made "cruder & simpler" in Marcuse's writings? Now I feel I must respond publically.

Come to Zurich! Daily swimming aids mental recuperation!

Warmly, Herbert

A public rift between us would be a calamity! Max's comments were taken out of context!

I do not underestimate the student movement -- it has interrupted the transition to a totally administered world (but it has a dram of madness).

Herbert, I really cannot come to Zurich. You have to reckon with a badly damaged Teddy. Quel monde! With warmest regards.

T.

SHORTLY AFTER HE WROTE THIS, ADORNO DIED OF A HEART ATTACK AFTER A CABLE CAR RIDE FROM ZERMATT UP INTO THE THIN AIR OF THE MATTERHORN.

CHAPTER 7

STEP BY STEP

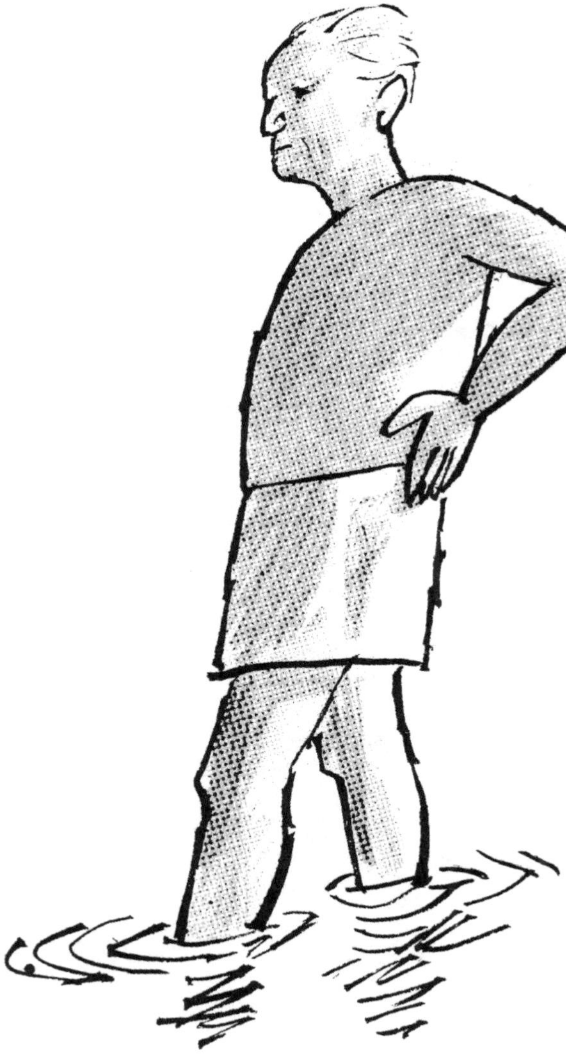

Panel 1 speech (Norman O. Brown and surrounding):

GIVE UP POLITICS FOR POETRY.

WE HAVE TO SURPASS THE ENLIGHTENMENT NOTION OF CHANGE.

INSTEAD OF CONFUSION, FUSION.

INDIVIDUALS ARE ILLUSIONS.

KINGDOMS ARE SHADOWS.

BACK IN THE USA, MARCUSE FOUND HIMSELF DEBATING TWO FIGURES WHO, LIKE ADORNO, HAD PROBLEMS WITH ACTIVISM.

WE LIVE IN A SOCIETY NO ONE CREATED & NO ONE WANTS.

TO SERVE A CAUSE WOULD BE TO SUBVERT THE CAUSE.

THERE IS NO REASON TO FIGHT ANYONE.

THERE IS NOBODY ON THE OTHER SIDE—

—ONLY THE MACHINE!

THERE IS NO REASON TO FIGHT THE MACHINE!

NORMAN O. BROWN

CHARLES REICH

NORMAN O. BROWN, MARCUSE'S OLD FRIEND FROM O.S.S. DAYS (SEE CHAPTER 4), OFFERED HIS TAKE ON EROS & UTOPIA IN *LOVE'S BODY.*

THE SELF IS AN ARTIFICIAL DIVISION OF OUR ORIGINAL ONENESS.

THE SELF MUST BE FOUGHT FOR, AGAINST THOSE WHO WOULD DISSOLVE IT INTO PRODUCTION & CONSUMPTION.

WE MUST RISE FROM HISTORY TO MYSTERY.

MEANING WHAT, THE EUCHARIST? THIS IS CALLED MYSTIFICATION.

HERE IS THE ROSE, HERE BEGINS THE DANCE.

UH HUH.

LOVE'S BODY

BROWN LIKENED THEIR DISPUTE TO A SIBLING RIVALRY, ROMULUS & REMUS QUARRELING.

CHARLES REICH'S POPULAR BOOK, THE GREENING OF AMERICA, CERTAINLY OUTDID MARCUSE IN THE OPTIMISM DEPARTMENT.

A NEW CONSCIOUSNESS HAS EMERGED LIKE FLOWERS PUSHING UP THROUGH CONCRETE.

AH, MORE FLOWERS.

IT IS **ALREADY** MAKING A REVOLUTION THAT WILL NOT REQUIRE VIOLENCE, & THAT CANNOT BE RESISTED BY VIOLENCE.

THAT WOULD INDEED BE SOMETHING NEW.

ITS REVOLUTIONARY VALUES ARE: DON'T HURT YOURSELF, DON'T JUDGE, & BE HONEST.

THESE ARE NOT NEW. WHAT'S NEW IS THAT, FOR THE MILITANT YOUNG, THEY ARE NO LONGER COMPATIBLE WITH REPRESSION, MISERY, & FRUSTRATION.

THE GREENING

SPEAKING OF VIOLENCE—

LIKE SHOOTIN' FISH IN A BARREL.

OK, LET'S BREAK FOR LUNCH.

MY LAI, 1968

OF THE HUNDRED OR SO SERVICEMEN WHO KILLED 300-500 CIVILIANS AT MY LAI, ONLY ONE WAS CONVICTED OF MURDER.

HE WAS ONLY FOLLOWING ORDERS

FREE RUSTY

THEY'RE ALL V.C.

AFTER TET HE GOT UPSET

IT COULD HAVE BEEN ME

AN OUTPOURING OF SUPPORT FOR LIEUTENANT WILLIAM CALLEY ELICITED AN ANGUISHED COMMENTARY* BY MARCUSE.

BEHIND THE POLITE DEBATES, THE REAL PEOPLE: MADLY IN LOVE WITH DEATH, VIOLENCE, & DESTRUCTION.

* IN THE NEW YORK TIMES, MAY 13, 1971

CALLEY SERVED 3½ YEARS OF HOUSE ARREST FOR HIS CRIMES, BUT AMONG HIS DEFENDERS THERE WAS MUCH TALK OF "HANGING."

I KILLED IN V.N. HANG ME TOO!

HE MAY WELL MEAN IT.

♪♫ SO GO AHEAD & HANG LT. CALLEY, JUST NAIL HIM TO THE CROSS 'CAUSE HE OBEYED ♪

EVERYONE KNOWS THERE ARE NO CIVILIANS IN VIETNAM

A MOST REVEALING STATEMENT— WAR AGAINST AN ENTIRE PEOPLE— A.K.A. GENOCIDE!

MARCUSE WAS PARTICULARLY UPSET BY THE CROCODILE TEARS OF SOME LIBERALS.

CALLEY IS ALL OF US! HE IS EVERY CITIZEN IN OUR GRACELESS LAND!

A COMPASSIONATE PARDON FOR CALLEY WOULD HEAL OUR WOUNDS & RESTORE OUR SOLDIERS' MORALE.

WOULD THAT INCLUDE THE THOUSANDS WHO MARCH AGAINST THIS GENOCIDAL WAR?

HOW ABOUT COMPASSION FOR THE VICTIMS OF THIS "MORALE"?

YES, A WHOLE LOT OF PEOPLE WERE REGRESSING TO A SIEGE MENTALITY IN RESPONSE TO THE MILITANT MOVEMENTS. THEIR HERO WAS CALIFORNIA GOV. REAGAN.

IF IT TAKES A BLOODBATH, LET'S GET IT OVER WITH!

NO MORE APPEASEMENT!

FIRST THING TO DO: FIRE ANGELA DAVIS!

DAVIS HAD JOINED THE COMMUNIST PARTY, JUDGING IT TO BE THE MOST SERIOUS OF ALL U.S. RADICAL GROUPS, SHORTLY BEFORE SHE GOT A TEACHING JOB AT UCLA.

REAGAN ORDERED THE REGENTS TO FIRE HER, WHICH THEY DID—TWICE! HER ACADEMIC FREEDOM BECAME A CAUSE CÉLÈBRE.

DAVIS WAS MORE INTERESTED IN ANOTHER CAUSE.

FACES SERENE & STRONG, BODIES DRAPED IN CHAINS.

THE JAILERS WANT TO IMPRESS UPON US THAT WE HAVE NOT YET ESCAPED FROM BONDAGE.

oners charged

THE "SOLEDAD BROTHERS"—JOHN CLUTCHETTE, GEORGE JACKSON, & FLEETA DRUMGO—WERE MILITANT PRISONERS CHARGED IN THE DEATH OF A GUARD. DAVIS & HER FELLOW ACTIVISTS ORGANIZED A DEFENSE CAMPAIGN.

DAVIS'S GROUP RECEIVED DEATH THREATS SO THEY ARMED THEMSELVES. THE WEAPONS WERE REGISTERED IN DAVIS'S NAME & STORED IN HER APARTMENT.

I KNOW YOUR BROTHER'S PROUD OF YOU FOR WORKING SO HARD ON THIS, JONATHAN—

—BUT YOU HAVE TO DO YOUR HOMEWORK TOO.

SAVE SOLEDAD BROTHERS FROM RACIST

END LEGAL LYNCHING

GEORGE JACKSON'S BROTHER WAS A JUNIOR AT PASADENA HIGH SCHOOL WHEN DAVIS BECAME FRIENDLY WITH THE FAMILY.

AUG. 8, 1970

JONATHAN JACKSON, JUDGE HALEY, & TWO OTHERS DIED IN THE SHOOTOUT, APPARENTLY AN ATTEMPT TO FREE JACKSON'S BROTHER & TWO OTHER CONVICTS HELD AT SOLEDAD PRISON.

POLICE ARE SEEKING AN ALLEGED CO-CONSPIRATOR THAT SUPPLIED THE ARMS JACKSON USED.

WANTED BY THE FBI

INTERSTATE FLIGHT, MURDER, KIDNAPPING

ANGELA YVONNE DAVIS

AGE: 25
OCCUPATION: TEACHER
RACE: NEGRO

CONSIDER POSSIBLY ARMED AND DANGEROUS

DAVIS SPENT TWO MONTHS AS A FUGITIVE FOLLOWED BY FOUR MONTHS IN CALIFORNIA JAILS BEFORE SHE COULD BE BAILED OUT. SHE WAS ACQUITTED OF ALL CHARGES IN JUNE 1971.

WHILE DAVIS WAS IN JAIL, MARCUSE JOINED THE WORLDWIDE CAMPAIGN FOR HER FREEDOM, AND WROTE TO HER:

DEAR ANGELA,

PEOPLE ASK ME HOW SOMEONE LIKE YOU COULD BE INVOLVED IN SUCH A VIOLENT EPISODE.

I DON'T KNOW IF YOU WERE INVOLVED IN THESE TRAGIC EVENTS BUT I KNOW YOU WERE INVOLVED IN THE FIGHT FOR THE OPPRESSED—

—AND THAT YOUR STUDIES TAUGHT YOU THAT YOUR WORLD OF CRUELTY & PERSECUTION (WHICH IS NOT MINE) COULD BE CHANGED & MUST BE CHANGED.

AND YOU LEARNED THAT THE PHILOSOPHERS OF WESTERN CIVILIZATION—THE VERY CIVILIZATION THAT ENSLAVED YOUR PEOPLE—WERE IN THE END ONLY CONCERNED WITH ONE THING

FREEDOM

YOU TOOK SERIOUSLY WHAT WAS FOR OTHERS MERE TALK.

YOUR CAUSE IS OUR CAUSE.

WHEN I WAS ASKED TO WRITE AN INTRODUCTION TO A LECTURE YOU GAVE ON FREDERICK DOUGLASS, I WONDERED AT FIRST: WHAT DOES YOUR PRESENT PLIGHT HAVE TO DO WITH PHILOSOPHY?

AND THEN THIS, FROM YOUR LECTURE:

FREDERICK DOUGLASS, SENT TO A "SLAVE-BREAKER"—

—STRIKES BACK!

THE SLAVE-BREAKER CALLS OTHER SLAVES TO HELP, BUT THEY REFUSE.

BUT THEN I READ THIS IN YOUR DISSERTATION PROPOSAL: "IN KANT, FORCE IS THE LINK BETWEEN THEORY & PRACTICE."

KANT

DOUGLASS

—AND SUDDENLY AN ABSTRACT CONCEPT CAME TO LIFE: FREEDOM IS NOT MERELY THE **GOAL** OF LIBERATION, IT **BEGINS** WITH LIBERATION. THIS, I CONFESS, I LEARNED FROM YOU.

90

HERE'S ANOTHER AREA WHERE MARCUSE LEARNED FROM DAVIS: **WOMEN & CAPITALISM** (THE TITLE OF AN ESSAY DAVIS WROTE WHILE IN PRISON).

HUMAN NATURE CAN BE DEFINED AS A CREATIVE INTERACTION WITH NATURE.

CAPITALISM REPLACES THAT INTERACTION WITH **ANTAGONISM**—

—AND FORCES WORKERS, ASSUMED TO BE MEN, TO SEPARATE THEMSELVES FROM NATURE.

WOMEN'S PRESUMED **CLOSENESS** TO NATURE, AS BEARERS & NURTURERS OF CHILDREN, CASTS THEM IN THE ROLE OF PROVIDING RESPITE FROM, & THUS MAKING POSSIBLE, CAPITALISM'S **DOMINATION** OF NATURE.

EQUALITY ALONE WILL NOT LIBERATE WOMEN. UNDER SLAVERY, BLACK WOMEN & MEN WERE **EQUALLY OPPRESSED.**

I CAN'T BREATHE.

WE DON'T TALK ABOUT THAT.

BUT IF EQUALITY MEANS WOMEN **COMPETE & DOMINATE** LIKE MEN, THEN WE FORFEIT OUR "NATURAL" RESISTANCE TO THE **PERFORMANCE PRINCIPLE.**

NONE OF THIS MEANS WOMEN MUST WAIT ON SOCIALISM FOR THEIR LIBERATION.

SNIP!

WOMEN MUST **BREAK OUT** OF THE FEMALE-MALE UNION—

—BEFORE WOMEN & MEN CAN COME TOGETHER ON A NEW & EQUAL BASIS.

91

HERBERT & INGE'S UNION WAS UNDERGOING SOME STRESS AROUND THIS TIME.

PROFESSOR! I NEED TO TALK TO YOU ABOUT MY DISSERTATION!

MY ARTICLE ON UNLEARNING OPPRESSION GOT ACCEPTED! WE SHOULD CELEBRATE!

HAVE I TOLD YOU ABOUT CO-COUNSELING? IT'S THE DEFINITIVE REBUTTAL TO FREUDIAN MISOGYNY!

RICKY'S OBSESSED WITH YOU, HERBERT. I CAN'T BEAR IT!

YOU HAVE TO TELL HER SHE CAN'T COME AROUND HERE ANYMORE.

IT WAS THE 1970s, & MANY A TEAR HAD TO FALL.

HIPPIES USE REAR ENTRANCE

Someday café

RECORDS

THE `SEVENTIES!

A DISAPPOINTING DECADE FOR MANY. LIBERATIONIST POSSIBILITIES (WHICH HAD NEVER BEEN MORE THAN A HINT, ACCORDING TO MARCUSE) DID NOT SEEM TO PAN OUT.

I WISH I KNEW HOW IT WOULD FEEL TO BE FREE

THE BOOMERS WENT THROUGH THE '60s & ALL I GOT OUT OF IT WAS THIS LOUSY TIE-DYE T-SHIRT

MARCUSE PINNED HIS HOPES ON THE WOMEN'S MOVEMENT.

WOMEN'S STUDIES CONFERENCE

THIS IS THE ONLY INVITATION TO LECTURE THAT I HAVE ACCEPTED ALL YEAR.

THE REASON IS SIMPLE. WOMEN'S LIBERATION IS THE MOST IMPORTANT & POTENTIALLY THE MOST RADICAL MOVEMENT WE HAVE.

THIS IS BECAUSE, AS ANGELA DAVIS SAYS, THE IDEOLOGY OF "FEMININITY" GIVES WAY IN WOMEN'S LIBERATION TO THE REALITY OF STRUGGLE AGAINST THE PERFORMANCE PRINCIPLE.

MARCUSE'S "MARXISM & FEMINISM" LECTURE OFFERS A WARNING, IN THE FORM OF A HISTORICAL DIGRESSION.

IN THE 12th CENTURY, THE ALBIGENSIAN HERESY PRACTICED FEMALE AUTONOMY, & IT WAS A WOMAN WHO DEFENDED THE HERETICS' LAST STRONGHOLD.

HOW WILL WE KNOW WHICH ARE HERETICS & WHICH ARE BELIEVERS?

KILL THEM ALL, LET GOD SORT IT OUT.

OVER 20,000 WERE SLAUGHTERED OR BURNED AT THE STAKE IN THE ANTI-ALBIGENSIAN CRUSADE.

MARCUSE BEGINS HIS 1972 BOOK, *COUNTERREVOLUTION & REVOLT*, WITH A LIST OF MORE RECENT MASSACRES.

300-400 STUDENT PROTESTERS SHOT IN MEXICO CITY 1968

1.3 MILLION CIVILIANS KILLED IN VIETNAM WAR

10 TO 40 THOUSAND BENGALIS KILLED BY PAKISTAN MILITARY 1971

UP TO 1 MILLION LEFTISTS KILLED IN INDONESIA 1965

1000 MASSACRED IN ASABA, NIGERIA 1967

HE ALSO MENTIONS

♪ 4 DEAD ♫ IN OHIO—

(I.E., THE ANTI-WAR STUDENTS SHOT BY NATIONAL GUARDSMEN AT KENT STATE U. IN 1970) — WHICH MIGHT SEEM LIKE A SMALL MASSACRE IN COMPARISON BUT IT HAD A HUGE IMPACT.

WE WERE ALL EXCITED ABOUT PROTESTING UNTIL KENT STATE.

THEN WE REALIZED— THESE GUYS AREN'T FOOLING AROUND!

NEVER BEEN TO A DEMONSTRATION SINCE.

"MICHELANGELO" WAS MY CO-WORKER AT THE NYC POST OFFICE IN 1971.

IN *COUNTERREVOLUTION & REVOLT*, MARCUSE REPORTS THIS EXCHANGE BETWEEN A RESEARCHER & A SMALL-TOWN MOTHER.

ANYONE WHO APPEARS ON THE STREETS OF KENT WITH LONG HAIR, DIRTY CLOTHES, OR BARE-FOOTED—

—DESERVES TO BE SHOT.

BUT YOU HAD THREE SONS THERE?!!

IF THEY DIDN'T DO WHAT THE GUARDS TOLD THEM, THEY SHOULD BE MOWED DOWN!

THE PEOPLE HATE THE REBELS WHO PERMIT THEMSELVES WHAT THE PEOPLE HAVE TO FOREGO & REPRESS.

93

ALONG WITH RECOGNIZING THE FEROCITY OF REACTION, *COUNTERREVOLUTION & REVOLT* CRITICIZES THE "CULTURAL REVOLUTION" FOR ITS FAILURES OF NERVE. JUST TWO EXAMPLES:

PETRIFIED RHETORIC

PETIT-BOURGEOIS DREAMER!

TROTSKYITE WRECKER!

CULTURAL APPROPRIATION

I GOT DA BLUES SO BAD I'M SMASHIN' MY GUITAR!

(MARCUSE DID NOT OBJECT TO WHITE ARTISTS PLAYING BLACK MUSIC, BUT RATHER THAT THE "GESTURE OF SORROW & INDICTMENT" WAS LOST.)

AT THE SAME TIME, THE BOOK HAILS THE 1970s SPREAD OF REBEL CONSCIOUSNESS BEYOND THE CAMPUSES.

THE YOUNGER WORKERS ARE NOT AS AFRAID OF LOSING THEIR JOBS AS THE OLDER ONES.

THEY COMPLAIN ABOUT THE UNION NOT MOVING FAST ENOUGH.

THEY EXPECT THE MANAGERS TO TREAT THEM AS EQUALS.

♪ TAKE THIS JOB ♪ & SHOVE IT!

THE COUNTERCULTURE OF THE 1970s WAS BROADER, IF NOT DEEPER, THAN THAT OF THE 1960s.

B-52 FAIR

WHAT COULD **WE** DO WITH THE $30 BIL. IT TAKES TO BUILD A BOMBER?

P.T.A.

ST. ANNE'S PARISH

OUR BODIES OUR SELVES

NEW ENGLAND FREE PRESS

DECENT SCHOOLS

JOBS & SHELTER FOR THE POOR

CLINICS FOR WOMEN

MILLIONS OF PAMPHLETS

FOR EX-STUDENT RADICALS LIKE ME, LIVING IN "BLUE-COLLAR" CITIES LIKE SOMERVILLE, MA, THESE WERE EXCITING TIMES.

DISCO, DISPARAGED BY RADICAL HIPPIES AS A RESURGENCE OF ARTIFICE & UPWARD MOBILITY, MAY HAVE BEEN ALL THAT, BUT IT WAS ALSO AN EXUBERANT ERUPTION OF QUEER, BLACK, & LATIN STREET CULTURE.

SADLY, ITS BLEND OF HEDONISM & MELANCHOLY FORESHADOWED THE GREATER COUNTERREVOLUTION TO COME.

MARCUSE'S TASTES WERE MORE ESOTERIC:

I CAN EXPLAIN THE STRUCTURE OF MY WRITING. I WAS ONCE IN A HOSPITAL, & IN THE ROOM NEXT DOOR A WOMAN, DYING OF CANCER, SCREAMED ALL NIGHT. THAT SCREAMING IS THE STRUCTURE OF MY WRITING.

A KINDRED SPIRIT

SAMUEL BECKETT

FOR MARCUSE AT THIS POINT, THE WOMAN DYING ALL NIGHT WAS INGE.

HE WROTE TO HIS FRIEND REINHART LETTAU:

"L'amour est fort comme la mort."— What a disgusting, contemptuous swindle.

THE PHRASE IN FRENCH IS FROM SONG OF SOLOMON 8:6 – "LOVE IS STRONG AS DEATH."

INGE DIED OF CANCER IN 1973.

HERBERT— ARE YOU ALL RIGHT?

CAN WE TALK NOW?

PETER MARCUSE & BILL LEISS RECEIVED SIMILAR PHONE CALLS.

UM— HOW WOULD YOU TAKE IT— WOULD IT BE OK WITH YOU— IF I WAS TO MARRY RICKY?

OF COURSE, DAD, IF THAT'S WHAT YOU WANT.

GOSH, JUST GO FOR IT. YOU KNOW WHAT'S BEST FOR YOU.

AND WE ALL KNOW OLD MEN DON'T LAST LONG WITHOUT COMPANIONSHIP.

RICKY, LIKE INGE, WAS A HARDWORKING ACTIVIST. SOME OF HER ACTIVITIES PUZZLED MARCUSE.

RICKY'S AT HER JEWISH SUPPORT GROUP TONIGHT.

WHY IS EVERYBODY SO INTERESTED IN THEIR TRIBE ALL OF A SUDDEN?

I DUNNO. ANTI-SEMITISM?

GEORGE KATSIAFICAS

REALLY? ARE THE JEWS IN DANGER?

WHERE HAVE YOU ENCOUNTERED ANTI-SEMITISM LATELY?

WHEN HAS ISRAEL EVER LOST A WAR?

JUST THE SAME, PEOPLE SEEM TO NEED TO FEEL THEY'RE PART OF AN OPPRESSED GROUP.

WHY DIDN'T PEOPLE NEED THIS IN THE MID-60s?

OH WELL, BACK THEN WE HAD "THE MOVEMENT" TO KEEP US WARM.

MARCUSE ELABORATED THESE CRITICISMS IN A 1975 LECTURE:

THE NEW LEFT'S STRENGTH—ITS DISTANCE FROM THE PRODUCTION PROCESS—WAS ALSO ITS WEAKNESS.

THE RESULT: ISOLATION, WITHDRAWAL INTO PERSONAL LIBERATION, THE TURN TO GURU-CULTS AS WELL AS THE FETISHIZING OF MARXISM.

MEANWHILE, THE UNLEASHING OF PRIMARY AGGRESSION RESULTS IN THE INTENSIFIED BRUTALITY OF EVERYDAY LIFE.

BRRAPP!

LIKE THE VICIOUS FARTS OF MOTORCYCLES!

MARCUSE TURNED TO THE FOLLOWING YEAR, & GOT AN UNUSUAL PRESENT.

FIRE HIM!

Dear Professor Marcuse:

UCSD will not of course cave in to political pressure regarding your employment.

You may not realize, however, that we recently set seventy as a mandatory retirement age. Out you go!

Sincerely,

William J. McGill
Chancellor

SEPARATED FROM ANY FORMAL CONNECTION WITH AMERICAN INSTITUTIONS, MARCUSE REVISITED GERMAN THEMES.

"DIE PERMANENZ DER KUNST"— YOU'RE WRITING THIS IN GERMAN?

THE LANGUAGE OF GOETHE, & HEGEL, & WAGNER.

RICKY & HERBERT COLLABORATED ON TRANSLATING THIS LAST BOOK OF HIS INTO ENGLISH.

IN THE AESTHETIC DIMENSION (1977) MARCUSE TURNS AGAIN, AS HE DID AFTER THE 1919 REPRESSION, FROM POLITICS TO **ART** AS THE UNASSAILABLE REFUGE OF FREEDOM.

THE AESTHETIC FORM EXCLUDES DOMINATION.

HOPES & DREAMS OF 1919, 1945, & 1968

BRECHT & BECKETT'S PLAYS ARE ONLY REVOLUTIONARY BY VIRTUE OF THE **FORM** GIVEN TO THE **CONTENT.**

LITERATURE CAN BE WRITTEN "FOR THE REVOLUTION" & STILL NOT BE **REVOLUTIONARY.**

IT IS ONLY REVOLUTIONARY TO THE EXTENT THAT IT PROVOKES **ESTRANGEMENT.**

IN THIS SENSE, BAUDELAIRE'S POEMS MAY BE MORE SUBVERSIVE THAN THE DIDACTIC PLAYS OF BRECHT.

THE BOOK GOES ON TO CRITICIZE "ANTI-ART" — THE URGE TO CIRCUMVENT FORM TO REVEAL TRUTH. MARCUSE ASSOCIATES THIS TREND WITH NEW YORK'S "LIVING THEATER."

WE WANTED TO DO "THE CONNECTION" BECAUSE IT WAS **REAL** WITHOUT FEIGNING "REALISM."

WE WANTED TO BE LIKE JAZZ MUSICIANS — NO DIFFERENCE BETWEEN ART & SELF.

EVERYONE'S HIGH & I'M NOT. YOU GAVE THEM MORE THAN YOU GAVE ME!

NOW WHY WOULD I CHEAT YOU, LEACH?

JULIAN BECK

JUDITH MALINA

1970s **FILM**, MORE THAN THEATER, EXPLORED FORM (GENRE) TO ACHIEVE ESTRANGEMENT.

YOU'RE SO NAIVE, MICHAEL! POLITICIANS DON'T KILL PEOPLE.

REALLY, KAY? MAYBE IT'S YOU THAT'S BEING NAIVE.

THE GANGSTER, THE COWBOY, & THE DETECTIVE ARE MADE REAL (& STRANGE) BY SITUATING THEM IN HISTORY.

WHATEVER ITS POLEMICAL AIMS, THE AESTHETIC DIMENSION QUICKLY VEERS OFF INTO THE PREOCCUPATIONS OF A NEWLYWED PHILOSOPHER APPROACHING THE END OF LIFE.

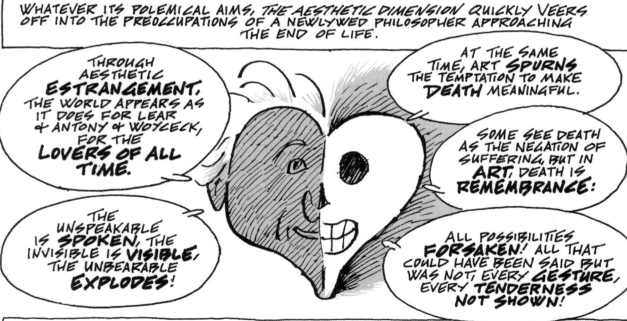

THROUGH AESTHETIC **ESTRANGEMENT,** THE WORLD APPEARS AS IT DOES FOR LEAR & ANTONY & WOYCECK, FOR THE **LOVERS OF ALL TIME.**

THE UNSPEAKABLE IS **SPOKEN,** THE INVISIBLE IS **VISIBLE,** THE UNBEARABLE **EXPLODES!**

AT THE SAME TIME, ART **SPURNS** THE TEMPTATION TO MAKE **DEATH** MEANINGFUL.

SOME SEE DEATH AS THE NEGATION OF SUFFERING, BUT IN **ART,** DEATH IS **REMEMBRANCE:**

ALL POSSIBILITIES **FORSAKEN!** ALL THAT COULD HAVE BEEN SAID BUT WAS NOT; EVERY **GESTURE,** EVERY **TENDERNESS NOT SHOWN!**

IT'S NOT HARD TO THINK OF POLITICAL "POSSIBILITIES FORSAKEN" IN THE COURSE OF A RADICAL LIFE, BUT WHERE WAS THE UNSHOWN TENDERNESS? (YOU WILL NOT GET AN ANSWER IN MARCUSE'S WRITINGS — HE TREASURED HIS PRIVACY.)

PERHAPS MARCUSE'S MARRIAGE TO RICKY FELT LIKE A CHANCE TO MAKE AMENDS.

DESCEND, OH NIGHT OF LOVE! RELEASE ME FROM THE WORLD! ♪

THEN AM I MYSELF THE WORLD! FREE OF ILLUSIONS! NEVERMORE TO AWAKEN! ♪

THE AESTHETIC DIMENSION MENTIONS IN PASSING THE THEME OF FORBIDDEN BUT CONSTANT LOVE, AS EXPRESSED IN RICHARD WAGNER'S OPERA "TRISTAN & ISOLDE."

WHEN I INTERVIEWED PETER & FRANCES MARCUSE, THEY HAD JUST COME FROM A SCREENING OF THE METROPOLITAN OPERA PERFORMING "TRISTAN."

MY FATHER LOVED THAT OPERA & NOW I UNDERSTAND WHY!

THE LONG NIGHT, WHEN THE KING IS AWAY UNTIL DAWN & THE LOVERS CAN BE TOGETHER & SING OF BEING JOINED ETERNALLY—

—THAT'S **EROS**! THE TIME OF TRUTH & TENDERNESS!

AND THANATOS IS **DAYLIGHT**: THE RETURN OF ILLUSIONS & OPPRESSION, THE RETURN OF THE TYRANT, BUSINESS AS USUAL!

"LIEBESTOD" IS THE NAME OF THE FINAL ARIA IN THIS OPERA.

DO YOU SEE, FRIENDS? DO YOU NOT SEE? HOW HE SHINES EVER BRIGHTER, SOARING ON HIGH, STARS ♪ SPARKLING AROUND HIM?

SHALL I PLUNGE BENEATH THEM, TO EXPIRE ♪ IN SWEET PERFUME?

TO DROWN, TO SINK UNCONSCIOUS- SUPREME BLISS! ♪

THE IDENTIFICATION OF "LIEBE" (LOVE) WITH "TOD" (DEATH) IN GERMAN ROMANTICISM REFLECTS THE SUPPRESSION OF "EROS" IN GERMANY'S MANY COUNTERREVOLUTIONS. YOU CAN SEE ITS APPEAL TO WAGNER, A VETERAN OF THE 1848 BARRICADES.

WAGNER WAS A MUSICAL REVOLUTIONARY AS WELL. THE OVERTURE TO "TRISTAN" IS IN NO KEY AT ALL!

OR RATHER, THE MUSIC MODULATES SO OFTEN THAT, RATHER THAN INDICATE EACH NEW KEY SIGNATURE, WAGNER WROTE OUT EACH NOTE AS A NATURAL OR A SHARP OR A FLAT.

with brother Erich

with Leo Löwenthal

80th Birthday

at the lake

haircut in our back yard

100

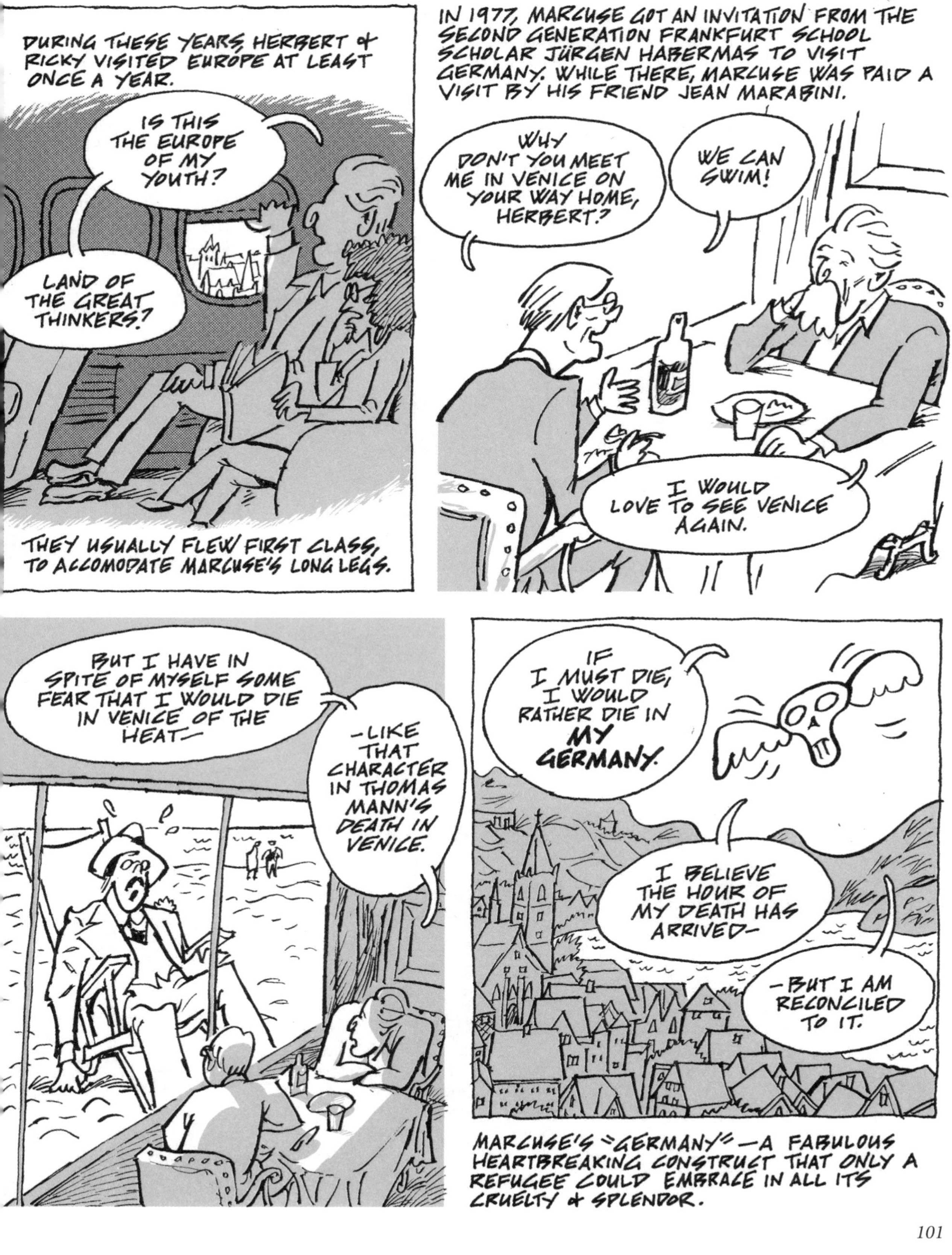
DURING THESE YEARS, HERBERT & RICKY VISITED EUROPE AT LEAST ONCE A YEAR.
IS THIS THE EUROPE OF MY YOUTH?
LAND OF THE GREAT THINKERS?
THEY USUALLY FLEW FIRST CLASS, TO ACCOMODATE MARCUSE'S LONG LEGS.
IN 1977, MARCUSE GOT AN INVITATION FROM THE SECOND GENERATION FRANKFURT SCHOOL SCHOLAR JÜRGEN HABERMAS TO VISIT GERMANY. WHILE THERE, MARCUSE WAS PAID A VISIT BY HIS FRIEND JEAN MARABINI.
WHY DON'T YOU MEET ME IN VENICE ON YOUR WAY HOME, HERBERT?
WE CAN SWIM!
I WOULD LOVE TO SEE VENICE AGAIN.
BUT I HAVE IN SPITE OF MYSELF SOME FEAR THAT I WOULD DIE IN VENICE OF THE HEAT—
—LIKE THAT CHARACTER IN THOMAS MANN'S DEATH IN VENICE.
IF I MUST DIE, I WOULD RATHER DIE IN MY GERMANY.
I BELIEVE THE HOUR OF MY DEATH HAS ARRIVED—
—BUT I AM RECONCILED TO IT.
MARCUSE'S "GERMANY"—A FABULOUS HEARTBREAKING CONSTRUCT THAT ONLY A REFUGEE COULD EMBRACE IN ALL ITS CRUELTY & SPLENDOR.

FOR ALL HIS ATTACHMENT TO HOMELAND, WHEN MARCUSE SUFFERED A STROKE LATER DURING THIS VISIT—

DIE GEDANKEN SIND FREI.

SPEAK ENGLISH PLEASE.

—HE FORGOT THE GERMAN LANGUAGE.

JÜRGEN HABERMAS REMEMBERS HIM SAYING NEAR THE END—

LOOK.

I KNOW WHEREIN OUR MOST BASIC VALUE JUDGMENTS ARE ROOTED:

IN COMPASSION, IN OUR SENSE FOR THE SUFFERING OF OTHERS.

HE DIED ON JULY 29, 1979.

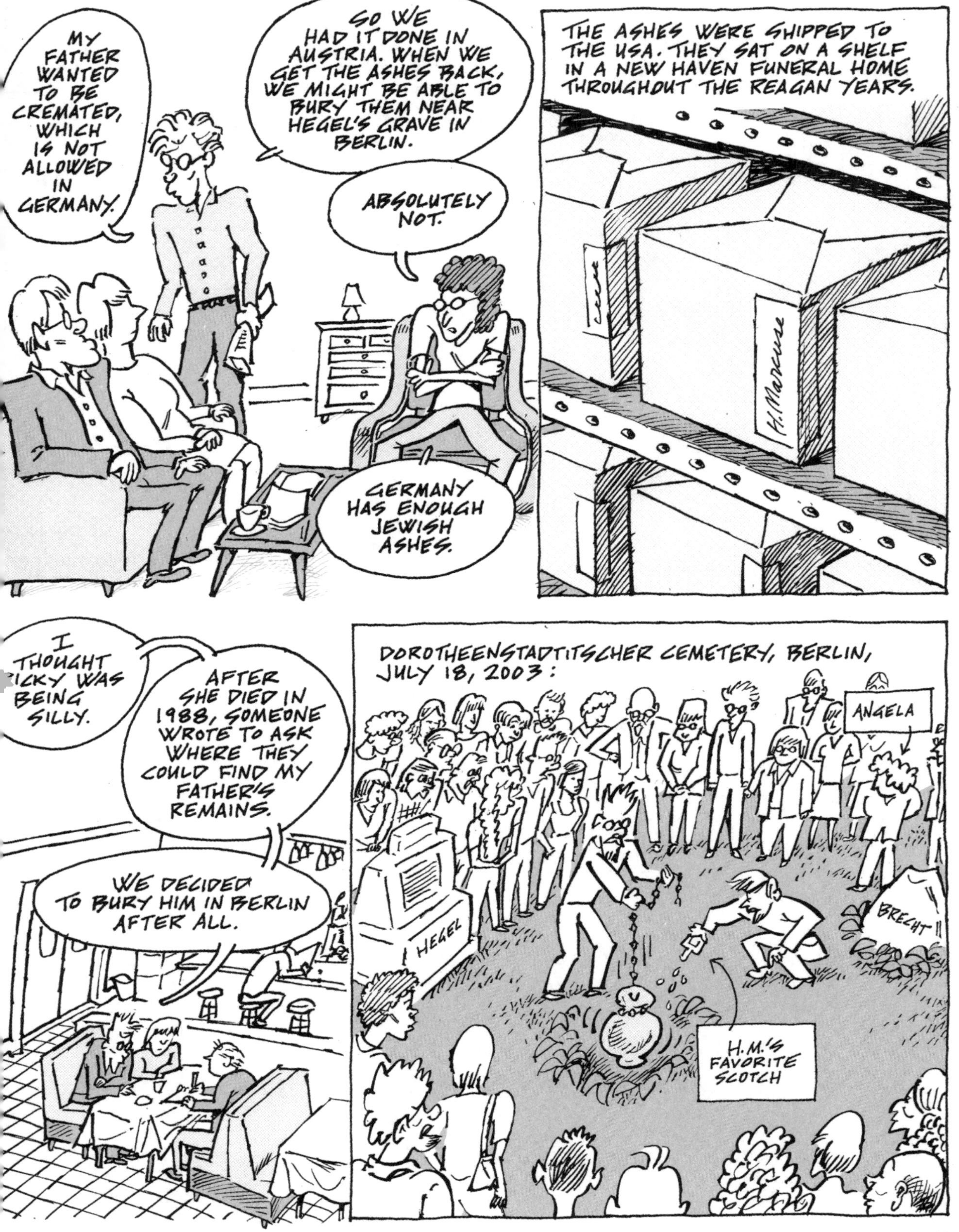
MY FATHER WANTED TO BE CREMATED, WHICH IS NOT ALLOWED IN GERMANY.
SO WE HAD IT DONE IN AUSTRIA. WHEN WE GET THE ASHES BACK, WE MIGHT BE ABLE TO BURY THEM NEAR HEGEL'S GRAVE IN BERLIN.
ABSOLUTELY NOT.
GERMANY HAS ENOUGH JEWISH ASHES.
THE ASHES WERE SHIPPED TO THE USA. THEY SAT ON A SHELF IN A NEW HAVEN FUNERAL HOME THROUGHOUT THE REAGAN YEARS.
H. Marcuse
I THOUGHT RICKY WAS BEING SILLY.
AFTER SHE DIED IN 1988, SOMEONE WROTE TO ASK WHERE THEY COULD FIND MY FATHER'S REMAINS.
WE DECIDED TO BURY HIM IN BERLIN AFTER ALL.
DOROTHEENSTADTITSCHER CEMETERY, BERLIN, JULY 18, 2003:
ANGELA
HEGEL
BRECHT
H.M.'S FAVORITE SCOTCH

A RECEPTION WAS HELD AT "BRECHT HOUSE" NEARBY.

THERE ONCE WAS A PHILOSOPHER NAMED HERBERT. THE SCHOOL HE BELONGED TO WAS FRANKFURT. HIS BODY WAS MADE ASHES BY US, ON HIS DEATH, NOT BY FASCISTS. HIS ASHES, NOT HE, ARE NOW COVERED WITH DIRT.

HERE ARE SOME MORE LINES IN HERBERT MARCUSE'S HONOR, WRITTEN ON THE OCCASION OF HIS 80th BIRTHDAY BY ONE OF HIS FAVORITE WRITERS, SAMUEL BECKETT.

IF I UNDERSTAND THE POEM, IT'S CONSISTENT WITH MARCUSE'S DECLARATION IN LONDON IN 1967: "NO ILLUSIONS, BUT EVEN MORE, NO DEFEATISM."

(FOR MORE OF THE LIMERICKS PETER MARCUSE COMPOSED FOR THIS OCCASION, SEE CHAPTER ONE.)

pas à part
(STEP BY STEP)

nulle part
(NOWHERE)

nul seul
(NOT A SINGLE ONE)

ne sait comment
(KNOWS HOW)

petits pas
(TINY STEPS)

nulle part
(NOWHERE)

obstinement
(STUBBORNLY)

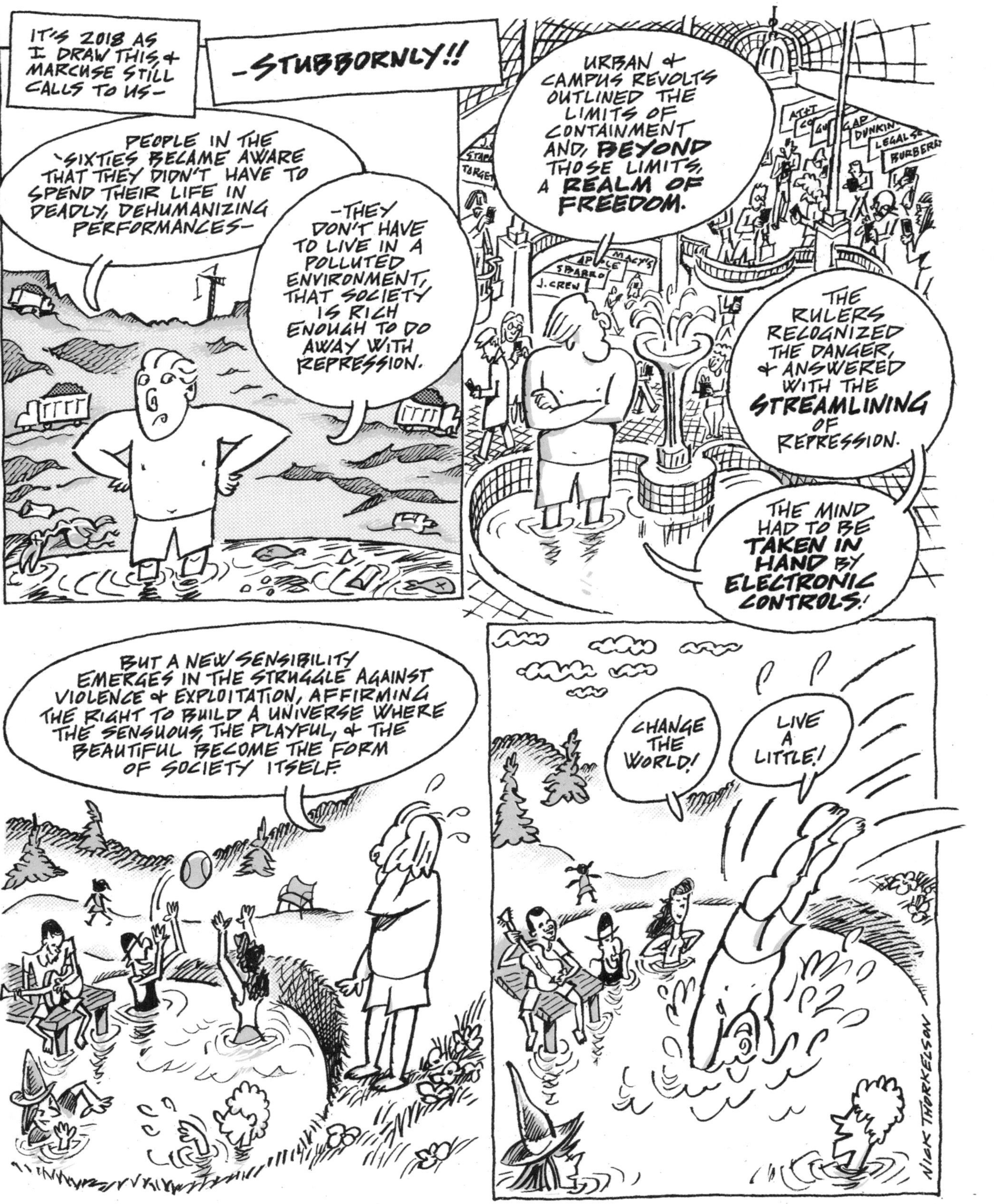

IT'S 2018 AS I DRAW THIS, & MARCUSE STILL CALLS TO US—
—STUBBORNLY!!
PEOPLE IN THE 'SIXTIES BECAME AWARE THAT THEY DIDN'T HAVE TO SPEND THEIR LIFE IN DEADLY, DEHUMANIZING PERFORMANCES—
—THEY DON'T HAVE TO LIVE IN A POLLUTED ENVIRONMENT, THAT SOCIETY IS RICH ENOUGH TO DO AWAY WITH REPRESSION.
URBAN & CAMPUS REVOLTS OUTLINED THE LIMITS OF CONTAINMENT AND, BEYOND THOSE LIMITS, A REALM OF FREEDOM.
THE RULERS RECOGNIZED THE DANGER, & ANSWERED WITH THE STREAMLINING OF REPRESSION.
THE MIND HAD TO BE TAKEN IN HAND BY ELECTRONIC CONTROLS!
BUT A NEW SENSIBILITY EMERGES IN THE STRUGGLE AGAINST VIOLENCE & EXPLOITATION, AFFIRMING THE RIGHT TO BUILD A UNIVERSE WHERE THE SENSUOUS, THE PLAYFUL, & THE BEAUTIFUL BECOME THE FORM OF SOCIETY ITSELF.
CHANGE THE WORLD!
LIVE A LITTLE!
NICK THORKELSON

AFTERWORD
Let a Thousand Flowers Bloom

Andrew T. Lamas

> A map of the world that does not include
> Utopia is not worth even glancing at.[1]
>
> —Oscar Wilde

The underlying structural reality of crisis-generating contradictions is unstable and unsustainable—creating opportunities for people to change the world. Amidst tremendous technological and productive capacities, humanity stands at a unique moment in its development—where liberating utopias and hellish alternatives are *realistic* possibilities.

> Today any form of the concrete world, of human life, any transformation of the technical and natural environment is a possibility, and the locus of this possibility is historical. Today we have the capacity to turn the word into hell, and we are well on the way to doing so. We also have the capacity to turn it into the opposite of hell. This would mean the end of utopia, that is, the refutation of those ideas and theories that use the concept of utopia to denounce certain socio-historical possibilities.[2]

For Herbert Marcuse, such an insight arises from the practice of radical interrogation known as *immanent critique*—challenging and subverting the present with its own alternative possibilities. This dialectical form of criticism is attentive to contradictions and to the dynamic potentialities (both liberatory and oppressive) that may arise amidst social instability. Politically, it implies a responsibility to "speak the truth to power."[3] It generates protest slogans such as "Demand the impossible!"—which, from a Marcusean perspective, means *demand that which the system has labeled impossible but which can be delivered through a reorganization of society's priorities and procedures.* As Marcuse wrote, "When truth cannot be realized within the established social order, it always appears to the latter as mere utopia."[4] So, the conventional understanding of utopia as an impossible project or a distant dream must be refused—based on the evidence of what is, in fact, possible now. It is in this sense that Marcuse is the anti-utopian philosopher of utopia.

For Marcuse, the future is unknowable but remains open to alternative realities as never before, and people can join in the struggle to make change; however, there are no guarantees as freedom is constrained and

1. Oscar Wilde, *The Soul of Man under Socialism and Selected Prose*, ed. Linda Dowling (London: Penguin Books, 2001). *The Soul of Man under Socialism* was originally published in 1891.

2. Herbert Marcuse, "The End of Utopia," *Five Lectures: Psycho-analysis, Politics and Utopia*, trans. by Jeremy J. Shapiro and Shierry M. Weber (Boston: Beacon Press, 1970), 62. "The End of Utopia," delivered by Marcuse as one of several lectures organized by the Sozialistischer Deutscher Studentenbund (SDS) at the Free University, Berlin, in July 1967, was first published in *Psychoanalyse und Politik* (Frankfurt: Europäische Verlagsanstalt, 1968).

3. The phrase is attributed to Bayard Rustin (from a letter he wrote in 1942). See American Friends Service Committee, *Speak Truth to Power*; Rustin was an unacknowledged coauthor of this book, as explained in the appendix to the book's 2012 edition.

challenged at every turn by a relentless storm of powerful, destructive forces.[5] As Marx famously wrote in 1852:

> [Humans] make their own history, but they do not make it as they please; they do not make it under circumstances chosen by themselves, but under circumstances directly found, given and transmitted from the past. The tradition of all the dead generations weighs like a nightmare on the brain of the living.[6]

Marcuse took this historical analysis very seriously and concluded that the struggle for freedom is impossible without the liberation of consciousness; but, liberated thought requires the nurturing of a free society beyond capitalism's one-dimensionality. Of course, as Marcuse was well aware, this situation lands us in the middle of an apparent paradox.[7] The Black radical tradition's powerful and moving articulation of this existential contradiction is sung in the blues, but always in the spirit of overcoming. As Angela Y. Davis writes:

> The insistence on imagining emancipatory futures, even under the most desperate of circumstances, remains—Marcuse teaches us—a decisive element of both theory and practice.[8]

In the historical record to date, oppression has always been met with resistance. As Frederick Douglass maintains, "If there is no struggle there is no progress. . . . Power concedes nothing without a demand. It never did and it never will."[9] Freedom's origin is not in abstract categories but rather in the praxis of affirmative negation. Ideas do not make change—but rather people struggling in solidarity to emancipate themselves. Domination from above has never been so total as to preclude challenges from below. The history of human struggle for liberation teaches that resistance has always been—and remains—possible. Despite tremendous barriers to critical understanding and radical praxis, resistance in its many forms—what Marcuse calls the Great Refusal ("the protest against that which is")—persists.[10]

> Social theory is concerned with the historical alternatives which haunt the established society as subversive tendencies and forces. The values attached to the alternatives . . . become facts when they are translated into reality by historical practice.[11]

In the spirit of radical solidarity, more than one hundred social theorists from around the world have joined together to offer reminiscences and reflections on Marcuse and his vital legacy of radical critique.[12] They have responded to this prompt:

"Marcuse, the philosopher _____."

4. Herbert Marcuse, "Philosophy and Critical Theory," trans. Jeremy J. Shapiro, in *Negations: Essays in Critical Theory* (Boston: Beacon Press, 1968), 143.

5. This latter image of the destructive storm is powerfully conjured by Marcuse's friend Walter Benjamin in his essay "The Concept of History" (first published in 1942, and also referred to as "Theses on the Philosophy of History"), inspired by Paul Klee's 1920 monoprint *Angelus Novus*. See thesis nine (IX) in Walter Benjamin, "Theses on the Philosophy of History," *Illuminations*, ed., Hannah Arendt, trans. Harry Zohn (New York: Schocken Books, 1969), 249.

6. Karl Marx, "The Eighteenth Brumaire of Louis Bonaparte," in *The Marx-Engels Reader*, ed. Robert C. Tucker (New York: W. W. Norton, 1978), 595.

7. Marcuse, "The End of Utopia," 80.

8. Angela Y. Davis, foreword to *Herbert Marcuse, Philosopher of Utopia: A Graphic Biography*, by Nick Thorkelson, ed. Andrew T. Lamas and Paul Buhle (San Francisco, CA: City Lights Publishers, 2019), vi.

9. Frederick Douglass, *Two Speeches by Frederick Douglass: One on West India Emancipation, Delivered at Canandaigua, Aug. 4th, and the Other on the Dred Scott Decision, Delivered in New York, on the Occasion of the Anniversary of the American Abolition Society, May, 1857* (Rochester, NY: C. P. Dewey, 1857), 22, available at https://www.loc.gov/resource/mfd.21039/?sp=22.

10. Herbert Marcuse, *One-Dimensional Man: Studies in the Ideology of Advanced Industrial Society* (Boston: Beacon Press, 1964), 63.

11. Ibid., xi-xii.

While each of the brief contributions presented below is uniquely revealing, collectively they offer a bouquet of insights about the multidimensional Marcuse. Let a thousand flowers bloom. May their thorns haunt all that oppress. May their scents tenderly affirm the transformative power of love on the march.

~

"Marcuse, the philosopher of Utopia and the Great Refusal who dreamed the Vietnamese and Third World Revolutions, the *long march through the institutions*, 1968, Women's Liberation, Sexual Liberation, Tahrir Square, Occupy, Black Lives Matter, the Bernie Sanders Campaign, and Trump Resistance.... *Viva!*" —DOUGLAS KELLNER

"Marcuse, whose Utopian system drew significantly, not merely on Plato, but fully as much on Proust (and Freud), to make a fundamental point about the memory of happiness and the traces of Utopian gratification that survive on into a fallen present and provide it with a 'standing reserve' [*Eros and Civilization*] of personal and political energy" —FREDRIC JAMESON

"Marcuse, the philosopher of revolutionary politics and radical aesthetics who always seemed to dance with the dialectic by emphasizing that the word *critical* in the term *critical theory* always and everywhere should be open-ended and preoccupied with self and social transformation, the critique of domination and contribute to the lasting quest for human liberation, remains—much like W.E.B. Du Bois, Frantz Fanon, and Amilcar Cabral—as relevant in the twenty-first century as he was in the twentieth century" —REILAND RABAKA

"Marcuse, the philosopher who never made peace with capitalist tyrannies: economic, political, cultural" —TARIQ ALI

"Marcuse, the philosopher who theorized an erotic braid of great refusal, deep desire, and radical collective possibilities—as if they were one" —MICHELLE FINE

"Marcuse, the philosopher and visionary thinker who sets the stage for what Audre Lorde will call the power of the erotic" —CYNTHIA WILLETT

"Marcuse, the philosopher who reminded us that Utopia is only what does not exist yet, rather than what cannot exist ever" —CYNTHIA A. YOUNG

"Marcuse, the philosopher who devised at least two indispensable concepts for a critical theory of present-day capitalism: repressive tolerance and the distinction between necessary and surplus repression" —NANCY FRASER

12. Each contribution has been expressly provided for this essay, except for those gathered from the following sources: Stanley Aronowitz, "Where is the Outrage? The State, Subjectivity, and Our Collective Future," in *The Great Refusal: Herbert Marcuse and Contemporary Social Movements*, ed. Andrew T. Lamas, Todd Wolfson, and Peter N. Funke (Philadelphia: Temple University Press, 2017), 364; Stanley Aronowitz, "The Unknown Herbert Marcuse," *Social Text*, no. 58 (Spring, 1999): 141; Judith Butler, *Gender Trouble: Feminism and the Subversion of Identity* (New York: Routledge, 1990), 131; Angela Y. Davis, in *Herbert's Hippopotamus: A Story about Revolution in Paradise*, a documentary film directed by Paul Alexander Juutilainen (Los Angeles: De Facto Fiction Films, 1996); Nancy J. Holland, "Looking Backwards: A Feminist Revisits Herbert Marcuse's Eros and Civilization," *Hypatia* 26.1 (Winter 2011): 71; Fredric Jameson, "Varieties of the Utopian," *Archaeologies of the Future: The Desire Called Utopia and Other Science Fictions* (New York: Verso, 2005), 7; Martin J. Beck Matuštík, Spectres of Liberation: Great Refusals in the New World Order (Albany: State University of New York Press, 1998), 105; Moishe Postone, *Time, Labor, and Social Domination: A Reinterpretation of Marx's Critical Theory* (New York: Cambridge University Press, 1993), 86n4; Rick Roderick, "Marcuse and One-Dimensional Man," *The Self Under Siege: Philosophy in the Twentieth Century* [lecture no. 4 in the 8-part video series] (Chantilly, VA: The Great Courses/The Teaching Company, 1993), https://www.youtube.com/watch?v=WNA-Kr1TQ0xc&t=535s; Slavoj Žižek, *Living in the End Times* (London: Verso, 2010), 78-79.

"Marcuse, the philosopher of revolutionary life" —ALEX CALLINICOS

"Marcuse, the philosopher who met the Καιρός—the Greek god of revolution— twice in his lifetime (November 1918 in Berlin, May 1968 in Paris) and tried to catch him in philosophical concepts" —ALEXANDER NEUPERT-DOPPLER

"Marcuse, the philosopher who theorized how late capitalism works to integrate and annihilate the revolutionary potential of life while also teaching us how delivering the goods to some is payment for a fascistic and repressive totality for all" —CLAYTON PIERCE

"Marcuse, the philosopher who once ran messages for Rosa Luxemburg and kept that audacious moment and its alternative future alive in all of his writing" —MIKE DAVIS

"Marcuse, the philosopher who—to his everlasting credit—mentored and inspired Angela Davis" —GERALD HORNE

"Marcuse, the philosopher who taught us to pay attention to the disruptive, transformative, and marvelous capacity of art" —ROBIN D. G. KELLEY

"Marcuse, the philosopher who—as the Friedrich Schiller of the Frankfurt School— believed that our drive for playful, aesthetically inspired cooperation is not to be permanently suppressed, can survive even the most powerful regime of political domination, and will come in some unknown future to its full realization" —AXEL HONNETH

"Marcuse, the philosopher of the post-capitalist Aesthetic State" —SAMIR GANDESHA

"Marcuse, the philosopher of negative thinking" —ANDREW FEENBERG

"Marcuse, the philosopher of political repolarization and generative conflict" —AK THOMPSON

"Marcuse, the philosopher of the negation of that which negates us" —CHRISTIAN GARLAND

"Marcuse, the philosopher of negation who helped me and a whole generation to say *No to Capital-Closure* and to whom I am delighted to say thank you for what you did" —JOHN HOLLOWAY

"Marcuse, the philosopher who taught us that you can't know Marx without Hegel, and you can't know either without an unquenchable thirst for freedom" —PETER HUDIS

"Marcuse, the philosopher who thought and lived the dialectics of revolution, from his work on Hegel, Marx, and dialectical reason in the 1930s-1940s, to his becoming the most revolutionary member of the Frankfurt School during the 1960s-1970s" — KEVIN B. ANDERSON

"Marcuse, the philosopher of postcapitalist society who developed the necessity-and-freedom dialectic in Hegel and Marx" —RUSSELL ROCKWELL

"Marcuse, the philosopher who developed the dialectical method in a way that permitted grasping the deepest-level dynamics of the historical situation with regard to their import for human liberation and happiness on the one hand and domination and misery on the other"—JEREMY J. SHAPIRO

"Marcuse, the philosopher who understood the *dialectical* aspect of critical thought and the necessity of grounding radical thought in the historical struggles of unfree people and whose writings were sterling models, and powerful inspirations, for my efforts to develop critical social thought in the interests of Black folks" —LUCIUS T. OUTLAW JR.

"Marcuse, the Marxist philosopher who opposes patriarchal civilization, with its dominant values of exploitation and repression" —KARLA SÁNCHEZ

"Marcuse, the philosopher who first investigated the relationship between surplus repression and surplus value production, a conceptual nexus which, half a century later, is still the starting point for queer Marxist thought" —HOLLY M. LEWIS

"Marcuse, the philosopher who, with his analysis of repressive desublimation and the masculinism of the Performance Principle, can explain the Incel movement" — WENDY BROWN

"Marcuse, the critical, Hegelian-Marxist, dialectical theorist of technology" —CHRISTIAN FUCHS

"Marcuse, the philosopher who argued that technology should be at the service of vital human interests" —JEFFERY NICHOLAS

"Marcuse, the philosopher of ecological crisis and revolutionary emancipation" —SARAH SURAK

"Marcuse, the philosopher of post-technological rationality" —MARCELO VIETA

"Marcuse, the philosopher whose vision of liberation from the *unfreedom* of technological civilization encompassed all of nature, including other animals" —JOHN SANBONMATSU

"Marcuse, the philosopher who saw the dialectical intertwining of animals and humans in both exploitation and liberation" —KATHERINE E. YOUNG

"Marcuse, the philosopher who elaborated the entanglement of science and technology with capital that remains the driving source of the rationality deficits of capital... and who, by the way, had a love of hippopotami because as they moved from land to water took on a wondrous lightness of being—a scintillating image of revolutionary change" —J.M. BERNSTEIN

"Marcuse, the philosopher of Struggle and Liberation" —SARAH LYNN KLEEB

"Marcuse, the philosopher of Liberation and Happiness" —STEPHEN ERIC BRONNER

"Marcuse, the philosopher of the New Sensibility" —ROBESPIERRE DE OLIVEIRA

"Marcuse, the philosopher of emancipation who realized that a conception of social-ism that excludes the dimension of Dionysian ecstasy risks perpetuating the contin-uum of domination" —RICHARD WOLIN

"Marcuse, the philosopher who defended radical desires against capitalism, consum-er society, and multiple repressions" —KOSTAS GOUSIS

"Marcuse, the philosopher who truly understood the scandal of qualitative difference, teaching us that for critical theory to be critical, it must exercise the power of the imagination"—ROBERT T. TALLY JR.

"Marcuse, the philosopher and prophet for whom the radical imagination was an essential element of revolutionary politics" —HENRY GIROUX

"Marcuse, the philosopher who imagined the social movements for peace and jus-tice as the polymorphous perversity of humanity's body politic" —RICHARD KAHN

"Marcuse, the philosopher of solidarity whose radical theory heralds the concrete imaginary of beautiful liberation" —EMRE ÇETIN GÜRER

"Marcuse, the philosopher of love unbounded" —VINCENT W. LLOYD

"Marcuse, the philosopher who defined socialism as a liberation of human sensitiv-ity"—JACK JACOBS

"Marcuse, the philosopher of the radical rather than the minimal goals of socialism"—CHARLES REITZ

"Marcuse, the philosopher of critical social theory and emancipatory political prac-tice"—PETER-ERWIN JANSEN

"Marcuse, the philosopher and keeper of the flame of radical humanism, emancipa-tion, and social transformation" —MICHAEL J. THOMPSON

"Marcuse, the philosopher of freedom" —IMACULADA KANGUSSU

"Marcuse, the philosopher of individual liberation, profoundly informed and influ-enced a generation" —ROXANNE DUNBAR-ORTIZ

"As Marcuse put it, *freedom* (from ideological constraints, from the predominant mode of dreaming) *is the condition of liberation,* in other words, if we change reality only in order to realize our dreams, without changing these dreams themselves, then sooner or later we will regress to the former reality. There is a Hegelian 'positing of presuppositions' at work here: the hard work of liberation retroactively forms its own presupposition." —SLAVOJ ŽIŽEK

"Marcuse, the philosopher of human emancipation" —TERRY MALEY

"Marcuse, the philosopher of how to create a just society of individuals with fulfilling lives" —HAROLD MARCUSE

"Marcuse, the philosopher of an alternative society that exists in the struggle for a radical democracy and the common interests of humankind" —WOLFGANG LEO MAAR

"Marcuse, the philosopher who insisted, at the most significant moments of his own exploration, that the telos of freedom remains self-perfection in a community with equals" —RICHARD LICHTMAN

"Marcuse, the philosopher who taught me that the future society of communist individuals begins in the struggle against existing relations of oppression, here and now" —WERNER BONEFELD

"Marcuse, the philosopher of the struggle for liberation and emancipation in all its forms"—EIRINI GAITANOU

"Marcuse, the philosopher who steadfastly hunted down the most brutal alienation that is manifest within the satisfaction of needs, the misery behind the abundance, the co-optation of criticism beneath progress, and the totalitarianism in rationality and efficiency" —CLAUDIA YARZA

"Marcuse, the philosopher who amidst the class compromises of the welfare state and 'mixed economy'—an era now so often contrasted positively with the neoliberal era—courageously insisted on the deep irrationalities and repressions embedded in the embrace of capitalist technology, media, and commodification" —LEO PANITCH

"Marcuse, the great critical theorist of liberation against the powerful forms of domination in advanced capitalist society" —CARL BOGGS

"Marcuse, the philosopher who happily made us conscious of how deeply we have internalized capitalist ideology and its irrational repression of a truly human society based on free association" —JOHN ABROMEIT

"Marcuse, the philosopher of defamiliarization and care" —CRAIG LEONARD

"Marcuse, the philosopher—a radical and a master of lucidity—from whom I learned a deep, critical approach to repressive tolerance" —SILVANA RABINOVICH

"Marcuse, the philosopher of labor who speaks of collusion, repressive tolerance, and anonymous power—lenses to see our own complicity in workplace repression"—CRAIG R. CHRISTIANSEN

"Marcuse, the philosopher who connected critical theory, psychoanalysis, and social movements" —JAN REHMANN

"Marcuse, the philosopher who expands Wilhelm Reich's exploration of the political and cultural unconscious by addressing the dialectical relation of alienated labor to the advent of consumer society, who—as a philosopher of praxis—was forever searching for openings for revolution and believed that theory was intimately linked to action, and whose most salient contribution to Critical Theory was to have shown the subsumption of reason under advanced capitalism to what he describes as 'technological rationality,' and to have demonstrated its profound implications for praxis" —STANLEY ARONOWITZ

"Marcuse, the philosopher who could imagine liberation not as power or possession, but as the pacification of existence, and who could bring the Critical Theory down to earth" —ASHER HOROWITZ

"Marcuse, the philosopher of total liberation—liberation of the mind, of the body, of all existence—and for whom philosophy is inseparable from politics" —DEBORAH CHRISTINA ANTUNES

"Marcuse, the philosopher who wrote the best commentary on Marx's *Paris Manuscripts* of 1844, a clear exposition of Marxian ontology, ready to become a political road map"—MARCO AURELIO GARCÍA BARRIOS

"Marcuse, the Hegelian-Marxist philosopher who wrote *Reason and Revolution*—the first critique of neoliberalism (*avant la lettre*)—and who planted seeds for a critical theory from the Americas" —STEFAN GANDLER

"Marcuse…continued to try to locate an immanent possibility of emancipation even when he viewed postliberal capitalism as a one-dimensional totality" —MOISHE POSTONE

"Marcuse, the philosopher who was always saying, don't give up on broad, radical visions for fundamental, sweeping social change, just because it doesn't seem to be on the agenda" —GAD HOROWITZ

"Marcuse, the philosopher who never gave up on the idea that emancipation is possible" —RAINER WINTER

"Marcuse, the realistic philosopher of the impossible dream" —GEORGE KATSIAFICAS

"Marcuse, the philosopher of possibility" —RAFFAELE LAUDANI

"Marcuse is the philosopher of hope when it faces hopelessness" —MICHAEL FORMAN

"Marcuse, the philosopher of hope, despair, anger, humanity" —NINA POWER

"Marcuse, the philosopher of *weitermachen*!" —HARRY VAN DER LINDEN

"Marcuse, the philosopher who had a sense of humor" —SUSAN BUCK-MORSS

"Herbert Marcuse, the imposing presence who teased me, just after I had published my first book on Kant's Critique, by proposing to Barrington Moore and me *A Critique of Pure Tolerance* as the title of our little volume, reassuring me when I objected that "No one will ever read it;" the Germanic philosopher who sat on the floor with my three-year-old son twirling a toy globe to show him the countries of the world; the world-historical presence who was that rarest of beings in the exalted realm of high theory and *Kulturkritik*; a good friend" —ROBERT PAUL WOLFF

"Marcuse, the philosopher who offered me a scotch when I came to interview him one afternoon in 1967, in the garden of Barrington Moore, Jr.'s house, and taught me that hedonism not asceticism is the revolutionary's true credo" —MARTIN JAY

"Marcuse, the philosopher who made it clear that the great cost of capitalism is the renunciation of genuine pleasure" —LISSETTE SILVA LAZCANO

"Marcuse, the philosopher who diagnosed fun as repressive desublimation and illuminated the erotic utopian potential in Freud's thought" —SHIERRY WEBER NICHOLSEN

"Marcuse, philosopher of the world and the underworld" —HEATHER LOVE

"Marcuse, the philosopher who understood that the real zombie apocalypse—way before it was a thing—was human alienation in one-dimensional society, and he helped us imagine how good liberation would feel, how revolution could bring us back to life" —NANCY D. WADSWORTH

"Marcuse, the philosopher who counseled militants to treat each other with *tenderness* in the prefigurative and scandalous work of growing *organs for the alternative* because, among other reasons, the *historical alternative* (the future) is already present in those subversive tendencies and forces we put into practice today." —AVERY F. GORDON

"Marcuse, the philosopher whose revolutionary zeal and incisive mind created an intellectual Molotov cocktail that was as feared by the privileged few as it was celebrated by the oppressed masses from around the world" —GABRIEL ROCKHILL

"Marcuse, the philosopher of today's resistance by rural migrant workers in China" —JENNY CHAN

"Marcuse, the philosopher feared by the U.S. intelligence agencies" —FILIP KOVACEVIC

"Marcuse, the philosopher of 'cultural Marxism' that the American Right still loves to hate" —JODI DEAN

"Marcuse, the philosopher of creative self-determination" —CHRISTOPHER HOLMAN

"Marcuse, the pathfinder who persistently illuminated why it is necessary for self-change and social change to be mutually constitutive, and of one piece in any revolutionary struggle against the technocratic rationality of capitalism and the calculated, mechanical, chord-chart precision of the forces of exploitation, hidden beneath a pity-charity narrative of helping the oppressed" —PETER MCLAREN

"Marcuse, the philosopher of a qualitatively better form of life for the least of these" —ARNOLD L. FARR

"Marcuse, the philosopher who taught us to pay attention to the 'other,' the 'outsider' and the 'subalterns' generally, and to cast our lot with them; and in *Eros and Civilization*, he gave us a vision of liberation, including our own" —CARL DAVIDSON

"Marcuse, the philosopher who predicted the flow of today's currents, where the one-dimensional man is the one who is truly incarcerated, while those behind bars hold the potential for true revolution" —TOORJO GHOSE

"Marcuse argues that a philosopher becomes concrete by rooting all critical categories in ongoing human struggles." —MARTIN J. BECK MATUŠTÍK

Marcuse, the philosopher "brings to Freud from Marx…the insight that scarcity, and hence repression, are not irreducible givens. What he…bring[s] to Marx from Freud is the insight that economic and political oppression is built on the basis of sexual repression" —NANCY J. HOLLAND

Marcuse, the philosopher who developed the "notion of an original and creative bi-sexual Eros subsequently repressed by an instrumentalist culture" —JUDITH BUTLER

"Marcuse, the philosopher of Eros's voice against the one-dimensional society"—SILVIO RICARDO GOMES CARNEIRO

"Marcuse, the philosopher whose theory of one-dimensionality projects flattenings of both material and cultural worlds (through the prism of what I call *one-dimensioning*), and not (as typically interpreted) their homogenization into a single, uniform dimension" —BEN FINE

"Marcuse, the philosopher of passionate teaching, generosity to students, and boundless, wicked humor" —William Leiss

"Marcuse, the philosopher who explained that as long as wealth is measured in terms of labor time, itself a function of the division of labor, alienation will exist; he restated the socialist's dilemma in terms of a struggle between the alienated and human needs in all of us; anyone who was the teacher and main influence on both Angela Davis and Abby Hoffman deserves the Left's version of the Nobel Prize: *HERBERT MARCUSE, PRESENTE*" —BERTELL OLLMAN

"Marcuse, the philosopher—*he blew our minds*: Like many young people in the new left of the 1960s, I was deeply influenced by this older German intellectual, whose books, especially *Eros and Civilization, One-Dimensional Man,* and *An Essay on Liberation* shaped our very American politics; his radical critical theory contributed to our lasting understanding of domination and liberation, to our *great refusal*" — WINIFRED BREINES

"Marcuse, the secular Jewish critical theorist and philosopher who remembered, through the power of pithy, clear writing rallied against idolatry, that liberation is the clarion call of responsibility for the ethical face of life" —LEWIS R. GORDON

"Marcuse, *the* philosopher of the 1960s…who caught the contradiction, the crisis that was always in the heart of modernity…who thinks that human beings as a species have historically accumulated potential to live a life with a good deal more freedom, and a good deal more happiness and solidarity than the one they live now…. Marcuse also never lost faith in the human species to reconstruct itself, to begin anew." —RICK RODERICK

"Marcuse, the philosopher of great refusals as preludes to a better world"—LAUREN LANGMAN

"Marcuse, the philosopher of the twenty-first century" —DAVID ROEDIGER

"Marcuse, the philosopher who was not only a philosopher" —MARCELLO MUSTO

"Herbert Marcuse taught me that it was possible to be an academic and an activist, a scholar and a revolutionary." —ANGELA Y. DAVIS

"Marcuse, the philosopher of multiple dimensions" —PETER MARCUSE

FURTHER READING

Selected Works by Herbert Marcuse

The Aesthetic Dimension: Toward a Critique of Marxist Aesthetics (Boston: Beacon Press, 1978).

"Charles Reich—A Negative View," *The New York Times* (November 6, 1970), 35.

Collected Papers of Herbert Marcuse, six volumes (New York: Routledge, 1998–2014), ed. Douglas Kellner (and Clayton Pierce on vols. 5 and 6): *Technology, War and Fascism* (vol. 1); *Towards a Critical Theory of Society* (vol. 2); *The New Left and the 1960s* (vol. 3); *Art and Liberation* (vol. 4); *Philosophy, Psychoanalysis and Emancipation* (vol. 5); *Marxism, Revolution and Utopia* (vol. 6).

"Correspondence on the German Student Movement" [1969], correspondence with Theodor W. Adorno, trans. Esther Leslie, *New Left Review*, issue 233 (January-February 1999): 123-136.

Counterrevolution and Revolt (Boston: Beacon Press, 1972).

"Dear Angela" [November 18, 1970, letter to Angela Davis], *Ramparts,* issue 9 (February 1971), 22.

The Dunayevskaya-Marcuse-Fromm Correspondence, 1954-1978: Dialogues on Hegel, Marx, and Critical Theory, ed. Kevin B. Anderson and Russell Rockwell (Lanham, MD: Lexington Books, 2012).

Eros and Civilization: A Philosophical Inquiry into Freud (Boston: Beacon Press, 1955); reprint with new preface (New York: Vintage Press, 1961); 2nd edition with new "Political Preface" (Boston: Beacon Press, 1966).

An Essay on Liberation (Boston: Beacon Press, 1969).

The Essential Marcuse: Selected Writings of Philosopher and Social Critic Herbert Marcuse, ed. Andrew Feenberg and William Leiss (Boston: Beacon Press, 2007).

Five Lectures: Psychoanalysis, Politics and Utopia, trans. Jeremy J. Shapiro and Shierry M. Weber (Boston: Beacon Press, 1970).

From Luther to Popper, trans. Joris de Bres (London: New Left Books, 1972).

Hegel's Ontology and the Theory of Historicity [1932], trans. Seyla Benhabib (Cambridge, MA: MIT Press, 1987).

Heideggerian Marxism, ed. Richard Wolin and John Abromeit (Lincoln: University of Nebraska, 2005).

"Heidegger's Politics: An Interview with Herbert Marcuse, by Frederick Olafson," New School for Social Research, *Graduate Faculty Philosophy Journal* 6:1 (1977): 28-40.

"Marxism and Feminism," *Women's Studies* 2.3 (1974): 279-288.

Negations: Essays in Critical Theory, trans. Jeremy J. Shapiro (Boston: Beacon Press, 1968).

One-Dimensional Man: Studies in the Ideology of Advanced Industrial Society (Boston: Beacon Press, 1964). Beacon edition with introduction by Douglas Kellner, 1991.

"On the Problem of the Dialectic" [1930-1931], *Telos* 27 (1976): 12-39.

Paris Lectures at Vincennes University, 1974, ed. Peter-Erwin Jansen and Charles Reitz (Philadelphia: International Herbert Marcuse Society, 2015).

Reason and Revolution: Hegel and the Rise of Social Theory (London: Oxford University Press, 1941); 2nd edition with new afterword (New York: Columbia University Press, 1954); paperback with new preface (Boston: Beacon Press, 1960).

"Repressive Tolerance," in Herbert Marcuse, Barrington Moore, Jr., and Robert Wolff, eds., *A Critique of Pure Tolerance* (Boston: Beacon, 1965).

Secret Reports on Nazi Germany. The Frankfurt School Contribution to the War Effort by Franz Neumann, Herbert Marcuse, and Otto Kirchheimer, ed. Raffaele Laudani (Princeton: Princeton University Press, 2013).

"The Social Implications of Freudian 'Revisionism,'" *Dissent* (Summer 1955). Note the response by Erich Fromm, "The Human Implications of Instinctivistic 'Radicalism,'" *Dissent* (Autumn 1955): 342-349; followed by Herbert Marcuse, "A Reply to Erich Fromm," *Dissent* (Winter 1956); and Erich Fromm, "A Counter-Rebuttal," *Dissent* (Winter 1956).

Soviet Marxism: A Critical Analysis (New York: Columbia University Press, 1958); paperback with new preface (New York: Vintage, 1961).

Transvaluation of Values and Radical Social Change: Five New Lectures, 1966-1976, ed. Peter-Erwin Jansen, Sarah Surak, and Charles Reitz (Philadelphia: International Herbert Marcuse Society, 2017).

"Watergate: When Law and Morality Stand in the Way," *The New York Times* (June 27, 1973), 39.

SECONDARY SOURCES

John Abromeit and W. Mark Cobb, eds., *Herbert Marcuse: A Critical Reader* (New York: Routledge, 2004).

Kevin Anderson, "On Hegel and the Rise of Social Theory: A Critical Appreciation of Herbert Marcuse's *Reason and Revolution,* Fifty Years Later," *Sociological Theory* 11.3 (November 1993): 243-267.

Stanley Aronowitz, "The Unknown Herbert Marcuse," *Social Text,* no. 58 (Spring 1999): 133-154.

John Bokina and Timothy J. Lukes, eds., *Marcuse: From the New Left to the Next Left* (Lawrence: University Press of Kansas, 1994).

Paul Breines, *Critical Interruptions: New Left Perspectives on Herbert Marcuse* (New York: Herder and Herder, 1970).

Wini Breines, *Community and Organization in the New Left, 1962-1968: The Great Refusal* (1982; New Brunswick, NJ: Rutgers University Press, 1989).

Mari Jo Buhle, *Feminism and its Discontents: A Century of Struggle with Psychoanalysis* (Cambridge, MA: Harvard University Press, 1998).

Paul Buhle, *Marxism in the United States: A History of the American Left,* 3rd ed. (London: Verso, 2013).

Javier Sethness Castro, *Eros and Revolution: The Critical Philosophy of Herbert Marcuse* (Boston: Brill, 2016).

Detlev Claussen, *Theodor W. Adorno: One Last Genius,* trans. Rodney Livingstone (2003; Cambridge, MA: Belknap Press of Harvard University Press, 2008).

Angela Y. Davis, "Abolition and Refusal," in *The Great Refusal: Herbert Marcuse and Contemporary Social Movements,* ed. Andrew T. Lamas et al. (Philadelphia: Temple University Press, 2017).

Angela Y. Davis, *Angela Davis: An Autobiography* (New York: Random House, 1974).

Angela Y. Davis, "Women and Capitalism: Dialectics of Oppression and Liberation," in *The Angela Y. Davis Reader,* ed. Joy James (Cambridge, MA: Blackwell, 1998), 161-192.

Angela Y. Davis, "Marcuse's Legacies" [1998 speech], reprinted in *The New Left and the 1960s,* vol. 3, *Collected Papers of Herbert Marcuse,* ed. Douglas Kellner (New York: Routledge, 2005), vii-xiv.

Jason Del Gandio and AK Thompson, eds., *Spontaneous Combustion: The Eros Effect and Global Revolution* (Albany, NY: SUNY Press, 2017).

Arnold L. Farr, *Critical Theory and Democratic Vision: Herbert Marcuse and Recent Liberation Philosophies* (Lanham, MD: Lexington Books, 2009).

Andrew Feenberg, *Heidegger and Marcuse: The Catastrophe and Redemption of History* (New York: Routledge, 2005).

Andrew Feenberg, "Remembering Marcuse," in Herbert Marcuse, *Philosophy, Psychoanalysis and Emancipation,* vol. 5, *Collected Papers of Herbert Marcuse,* ed. Douglas Kellner and Clayton Pierce. (London: Routledge, 2011), 234-241.

Christian Fuchs, *Emanzipation! Technik und Politik bei Herbert Marcuse* (Aachen: Shaker, 2005).

Christian Fuchs, *Herbert Marcuse interkulturell gelesen* (Nordhausen: Bautz, 2005).

Gad Horowitz, *Repression—Basic and Surplus Repression in Psychoanalytic Theory: Freud, Reich, and Marcuse* (Toronto: University of Toronto Press, 1977).

Martin Jay, *The Dialectical Imagination: A History of the Frankfurt School and the Institute of Social Research, 1923-1950* (Little, Brown, 1973).

George Katsiaficas, *The Subversion of Politics: European Autonomous Social Movements and the Decolonization of Everyday Life* (Atlantic Highlands, NJ: Humanities Press, 1997).

George Katsiaficas, *The Imagination of the New Left: A Global Analysis of 1968* (Boston: South End Press, 1987).

George Katsiaficas, "Marcuse's Cognitive Interest: A Personal View," *New Political Science* 18.2-3 (1996): 159-170; reprinted as "Marcuse as Activist: Reminiscences on his Theory and Practice," in Herbert Marcuse, *The New Left and the 1960s*, vol. 3, *Collected Papers of Herbert Marcuse,* ed. Douglas Kellner (London: Routledge, 2005), 192-203.

Barry Katz, *Herbert Marcuse and the Art of Liberation: An Intellectual Biography* (London: New Left Books, 1982).

Douglas Kellner, *Herbert Marcuse and the Crisis of Marxism* (Berkeley: University of California Press, 1984).

Douglas Kellner, Tyson E Lewis, and Clayton Pierce, *On Marcuse: Critique, Liberation, and Reschooling in the Radical Pedagogy of Herbert Marcuse* (Rotterdam: Sense Publishers, 2008).

Andrew T. Lamas, Todd Wolfson, and Peter N. Funke, eds., *The Great Refusal: Herbert Marcuse and Contemporary Social Movements* (Philadelphia: Temple University Press, 2017).

William Leiss, "Modern Science, Enlightenment, and the Domination of Nature: No Exit?," in *Critical Ecologies: The Frankfurt School and Contemporary Environmental Crises,* ed. Andrew Biro (Toronto: University of Toronto Press, 2011), 23-42.

Karl Löwith, "The Political Implications of Heidegger's Existentialism," trans. Richard Wolin, in *The Heidegger Controversy: A Critical Reader,* ed. Richard Wolin (Cambridge, MA: MIT Press, 1993), 167-185. Written in 1939, it first appeared as "Les implications politiques de la philosophie de l'existence chez Heidegger," in *Les Temps Modernes* 14 (1946-1947).

Timothy J. Lukes, *Flight Into Inwardness: An Exposition and Critique of Herbert Marcuse's Theory of Liberative Aesthetics* (London: Associated University Presses, 1985).

Terry Maley, ed., *One-Dimensional Man 50 Years On: The Struggle Continues* (Winnipeg: Fernwood, 2017).

Paul Mattick, *Critique of Marcuse: One-Dimensional Man in Class Society* (London: Merlin Press, 1972).

Robert Pippin, Andrew Feenberg, Charles P. Webel, eds., *Marcuse: Critical Theory and the Promise of Utopia* (South Hadley, MA: Bergin & Garvey Publishers, 1988).

Charles Reitz, *Art, Alienation, and the Humanities: A Critical Engagement with Herbert Marcuse* (Albany: State University of New York Press, 2000).

Charles Reitz, *Crisis and Commonwealth: Marcuse, Marx, McLaren* (Lanham, MD: Lexington Books, 2013).

Charles Reitz, *Ecology and Revolution: Herbert Marcuse and the Challenge of a New World System Today* (London: Routledge, 2019).

Morton Schoolman, *The Imaginary Witness: The Critical Theory of Herbert Marcuse* (New York: New York University Press, 1984).

Jennifer Schuessler, "Heidegger's Notebooks Renew Focus on Anti-Semitism," *New York Times* (March 30, 2014), C1.

David Norman Smith, "Introduction to Herbert Marcuse, 'On the Critique of Sociology,'" *Mid-American Review of Sociology* 16.2 (Spring 1992): 1-13.

Kurt H. Wolff and Barrington Moore Jr., eds., *The Critical Spirit: Essays in Honor of Herbert Marcuse* (Boston: Beacon Press, 1967).

Richard Wolin, *Heidegger's Children: Hannah Arendt, Karl Löwith, Hans Jonas, and Herbert Marcuse* (Princeton, NJ: Princeton University Press, 2001).

Selected Films and Videos:

Camel Collective, *La distancia entre Pontresina y Zermatt es la misma que la de Zermatt a Pontresina = The Distance from Pontresina to Zermatt is the Same as the Distance from Zermatt to Pontresina* (Ciudad de México: MUAC, El Museo Universitario Arte Contemporáneo, UNAM, 2017), video excerpt: www.youtube.com/watch?v=KS_6L8A4AfM&feature=youtu.be.

Andrew Feenberg, "The Essential Marcuse," lecture in La Jolla, CA, August 24, 2007 (San Diego, CA: UCSD-TV and D. G. Wills Books, 2007), www.youtube.com/watch?v=nFbypIr4RmQ&t=510s.

Paul Alexander Juutilainen, *Herbert's Hippopotamus: Marcuse and Revolution in Paradise* (Los Angeles, CA: De Facto Fiction Films, 1996), www.youtube.com/watch?v=gbzhmMDFcFQ.

Herbert Marcuse, interview by Bryan Magee, on "Modern Philosophy: Herbert Marcuse and the Frankfurt School," (London: BBC, 1977), www.youtube.com/watch?v=2pzfy2izu44.

Herbert Marcuse, interview by Helen Hawkins, on "Viewpoints," April 25, 1979 (San Diego, CA: KPBS-TV, 1979), www.youtube.com/watch?v=XhzKyvLbY8M.

Rick Roderick, "Marcuse and *One-Dimensional Man*," *The Self Under Siege: Philosophy in the Twentieth Century* [lecture no. 4 in the 8-part video series] (Chantilly, VA: The Great Courses, The Teaching Company, 1993), www.youtube.com/watch?v=WNAKr1TQ0xc&t=535s.

Peter Villon, *Dialectics of Liberation* (Vancouver: Villon Films, 1967). Herbert Marcuse's lecture ("Liberation from the Affluent Society") is featured in the documentary, and the transcript is available at www. marcuse.org/herbert/publications. Video excerpts of Marcuse's lecture at the Dialectics of Liberation conference in London, July 28, 1967, www.youtube.com/watch?v=bQLpqno-6J_g&t=142s.

Selected Journals—Special Issues on Marcuse and His Legacy for Today

"Critical Refusals," Part 1/Part 2, ed. Andrew T. Lamas, Douglas Kellner, Charles Reitz, and Arnold L. Farr, *Radical Philosophy* Review 16.1 (2013)/16.2 (2013).

"Refusing One-Dimensionality," Part 1/Part 2, ed. Andrew T. Lamas, *Radical Philosophy Review* 19.1 (2016) / 20.1 (2017).

"Marcuse in the Twenty-First Century: Radical Politics, Critical Theory, and Revolutionary Praxis," ed. Robert Kirsch and Sarah Surak, *New Political Science* 38.4 (2017).

Selected Websites:

Herbert Marcuse Official Homepage (ed. Harold Marcuse): www.marcuse.org/herbert/

International Herbert Marcuse Society: www.MarcuseSociety.org